Brachysynodontis batensoda

Synodontis schoutedeni

A FISHKEEPER'S GUIDE TO

AFRICAN & ASIAN CATFISHES

A detailed exploration of these intriguing and highly
collectable fishes, featuring 50 species

David Sands

Tetra Press

No. 16067

A Salamander Book

Synodontis ocellifer

Credits

Editor: Geoff Rogers   Designer: Tony Dominy
Colour reproductions:
Rodney Howe Ltd.
Filmset: SX Composing Ltd.
Printed in Belgium by Henri Proost & Cie, Turnhout.

Author

A combination of practical experience and academic research has made David Sands ideally qualified to present this survey of African and Asian catfishes. As an importer and retailer of tropical freshwater and marine fishes, Mr Sands has encountered at first hand all the challenges which face the fishkeeper. Renowned internationally for his authoritative series of volumes on Catfishes of the World and a regular contributor to leading aquarist magazines in the UK and USA, he can advise both accomplished and aspiring fishkeepers how to keep and enjoy these intriguing fishes.

Contents

Introduction 8

Aquarium selection 10

Water requirements and filtration 16

Lighting and heating 22

Aquascaping 24

Feeding and routine maintenance 28

Basic health care 32

Breeding 36

Species section 38
A photographic survey of 55 species
of African and Asian catfishes

Index 76

Picture credits 77

Introduction

Almost every tropical freshwater community aquarium contains catfishes. The fact that many are nocturnal and secretive by nature serves only to increase their fascination to aquarists. Beginners are invariably encouraged to introduce a few catfishes to their first system; as substrate feeders they are promoted as 'aquarium cleaners'. The myth that they are simply scavengers content to survive on the 'scraps from other fishes' tables' is one that should have long since passed into folklore. If the more robust catfishes are starved of their correct diet then this will simply sharpen their nocturnal instinct to predate on slow and weak fishes. A good many shoals of Neon Tetras have disappeared overnight for this reason. The importance of correct feeding is considered on pages 28-30.

African and Asian catfishes have a great deal to offer aquarists in terms of diversity, size, behaviour and, most of all, hardiness. Many have adapted to live in extreme environments, such as swift

mountain streams or stagnant muddy pools. Not surprisingly, their hardy nature and adaptibility enables them to survive the rigours of transportation across the world, with the changes in water quality and periods of overcrowding such journeys entail.

Correct identification can be a problem with many species. The fish farmers in Singapore, Hong Kong and Bangkok are more familiar with the larger food fishes than with the aquarium species. Thus, many catfishes destined for the aquarium trade, although known by native names, are not identified in terms of a scientific name. As an example, the popular Asian catfish *Mystus micracanthus* is given an African 'scientific' name of *Synodontis* by commercial exporters. Most species are not extensively described in commercial literature, however, and, perversely, this paucity of information has encouraged an even more enthusiastic interest among fishkeepers around the world.

Aquarium selection

Because of the wide size range of catfishes, almost any standard aquarium can house representatives of this group.

Community aquariums
Most catfishes are chosen for established community aquariums. For small systems of 45x38x30cm (18x15x12in) or 60x38x30cm (24x15x12in), the following dwarf species are easy to accommodate in small groups. Aquarium measurements refer to length, depth and width respectively.

African
Riverine
Mochokiella paynei
Synodontis aterrimus
Synodontis nigriventris
Synodontis robertsi
Chiloglanis cameronensis

Rift Valley Lake
Synodontis eurystomus
Synodontis petricolor

Asian
Kryptopterus bicirrhis
Leiocassis stenomus
Mystus micracanthus

In the African grouping, *Synodontis nigriventris* is readily available in aquarist shops. The other species are seasonal and in some cases, such as the dwarf *Synodontis* from the Rift Valley Lakes, quite expensive.

The above species should be considered acceptable for small community systems, although in the case of the smaller members of the *Bagridae* family, such as *Leiocassis* and *Mystus*, it is wise to note that even these species will predate on small fish. *Synodontis*, by contrast, are rarely predatory towards fishes, so the majority are considered ideal catfishes for small aquariums.

Catfish aquariums
The ideal aquarium set up specifically for catfishes should have a large substrate area in which the fishes can establish territories and occupy daytime hiding places. The water depth is almost immaterial, since these scavenging fishes will spend much of their time on or close to the bottom. This requirement can save money, since aquarium costs are determined by the size and amount of glass used, and shallow aquariums require a lighter gauge of glass than deeper tanks as a general rule.

The average aquarium system measures 90x38x30cm (36x15x12in). For a catfish aquarium the ideal width (i.e. front to back measurement) of such a system would be 38cm (15in) or 45cm (18in), or even 60cm (24in). Because the depth is not increased, the extra cost for glass would be marginal and the cost of silicone sealant would be negligible. The same lighting would be required, although a larger canopy could cost slightly more.

The only drawback to a wide aquarium may be purely practical: if it is raised high off the ground then reaching to the back for planting or general maintenance could be difficult. Also on the practical front; in wider systems, it may be more convenient to fit undergravel filter plates widthways rather than lengthways. (See also page 18 for advice on water quality and filtration in catfish aquariums.)

Large systems are usually based on tank measurements of 120x38x30cm (48x15x12in) or 120x45x30cm (48x18x12in) and here again the narrow widths restrict the extent of the substrate and the structure of the aquascaping. In such narrow tanks, it is simply not possible to build extensive cave structures or include large pieces of bogwood. Merely increasing the width to 38cm (15in) allows bogwood and rocks to be spaced out more usefully. With the larger spiny catfishes, a great deal of damage can be caused when fishes dispute the same cave or bogwood underside. The catfishes do not necessarily bite each other, it is simply that in the jostling for space

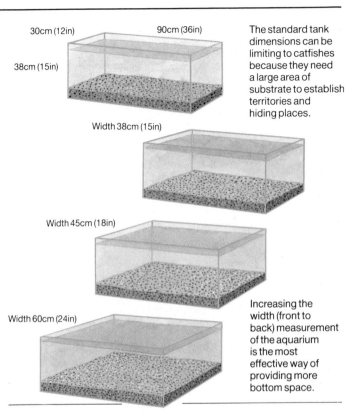

30cm (12in)   90cm (36in)

38cm (15in)

The standard tank dimensions can be limiting to catfishes because they need a large area of substrate to establish territories and hiding places.

Width 38cm (15in)

Width 45cm (18in)

Width 60cm (24in)

Increasing the width (front to back) measurement of the aquarium is the most effective way of providing more bottom space.

the outspread sharp spines scratch their scaleless bodies.

If groups of small catfishes are grown up together in a spacious, well-aquascaped system they are more likely to breed, although African and Asian catfishes have always proved difficult in this respect, even for the most experienced fishkeepers.

Siting a catfish aquarium
Catfishes are extremely sensitive to vibrations and thus easily disturbed. To be able to watch them successfully, therefore, it is important to cushion the aquarium from sound and vibrations as far as possible and to set it on a firm stand on a solid surface. A wooden floor with a cavity beneath the floorboards, for example, can transmit the vibration of footsteps to the tank and disturb the fishes. Even carpeting the floor may not completely eliminate the problem. A

solid floor is preferable because it does not transmit vibrations to the same extent. Metal stands are liable to transmit vibrations to the tank more easily than, say, a well-built wooden one, irrespective of the type of floor on which they are placed.

Siting the aquarium correctly is extremely important because, once frightened, catfishes tend to become nervous and will not venture out into the open. Almost all catfishes are nocturnal, spending little time swimming out in the open during daylight hours. If they are constantly disturbed by vibrations reaching the aquarium, this already restricted opportunity to view them will be reduced to almost nothing.

Catfishes owe their exceptional hypersensitivity to sounds and vibrations to two separate detection systems working in harmony. One is the lateral line system, which is common to all fishes and acts almost like an external nervous system located along the flanks. The other system is the so-called Weberian apparatus (also seen in Carp, Characins and Loaches) in which the swimbladder acts as a 'sound radar' and sends signals to the nervous system. It is not surprising, therefore, that catfishes are so alert to their surroundings and that selecting and siting their aquariums need such careful consideration to achieve success.

Above: *Unlike most catfishes, the Asian Glass Catfish* (Kryptopterus bicirrhis) *has adapted to a life in the upper water levels. It swims at a head-up angle by constant movements of its anal fin and tail.*

Below: *This table acts as a guide to the water capacity of standard-sized tanks. It is extremely important to know the tank capacity when assessing stocking levels, particularly in the case of catfishes.*

TANK CAPACITIES

Size (L×D×W)	Litres	Imp. Gallons	US Gallons
60×38×30 cm (24×15×12 in)	68	15	18.0
90×38×30 cm (36×15×12 in)	96	21	25.2
120×45×38 cm (48×18×15 in)	195	43	51.6
180×45×45 cm (72×18×18 in)	373	82	98.4

GUIDE TO STOCKING LEVELS

Type of fish	Volume of water required per fish		
	Litres	Imp. Gallons	US Gallons
Small midwater fishes (Tetras, rasboras etc.)	1.1	0.25	0.33
Medium-sized midwater fishes (Barbs, larger tetras, gouramis, etc.)	2.3	0.5	0.6
Catfishes (10-15 cm/4-6 in)	23.0	5.0	6.0

Above: *Stocking levels are often calculated on the basis of surface area of water per unit length of fish. This table provides a guide on the basis of water volume per fish. It shows that catfishes clearly require a relatively large volume of water compared with other familiar fishes in a freshwater aquarium.*

Below: *This table lists a selection of fishes suitable for a community system and, using the water volume per fish figures quoted above, shows the ideal tank size required. At first glance, the system appears understocked, but the quotas allow for the fishes to live in harmony and mature to breeding size.*

GUIDE TO REQUIRED SIZE OF TANK

Type of fish	Volume of water required by fishes		
	Litres	Imp. Gallons	US Gallons
10 Tiger Barbs (*Barbus tetrazona tetrazona*)	23.0	5.0	6.0
5 Pearl Gouramis (*Trichogaster leeri*)	11.5	2.5	3.0
10 Bleeding Heart Tetras (*Hyphessobrycon erythrostigma*)	23.0	5.0	6.0
5 Catfishes (e.g. 2 *Mystus* sp. plus 3 *Leiocassis* sp. at 10-15 cm/4-6 in)	115.0	25.0	30.0
Total volume of water required	**172.5**	**37.5**	**45.0**

Therefore use the nearest size tank with a capacity of 195 litres (43 Imp./51.6 US Gallons) measuring 120×45×38 cm (48×18×15 in).

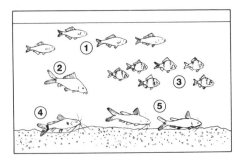

Aquarium size 60×38×30cm (24×15×12in)

Key
1 *Danio malabaricus*
2 *Labeo bicolor*
3 *Barbus tetrazona*
4 *Mystus micracanthus*
5 *Leiocassis siamensis*
6 *Trichogaster leeri*
7 *Kryptopterus bicirrhis*
8 *Barbus nigrofasciatus*
9 *Epalzeorhynchus kallopterus*

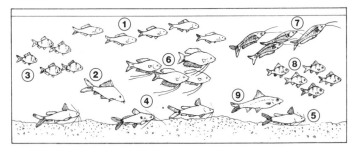

Aquarium size 90×38×30cm (36×15×12in)

AFRICAN

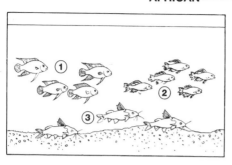

Aquarium size 60×38×30cm (24×15×12in)

Key
1 *Hemichromis thomasi*
2 *Phenacogrammus interruptus*
3 *Synodontis aterrimus*
4 *Pelvicachromis pulcher (Kribensis)*
5 *Arnoldichthys spilopterus*
6 *Eutropiellus vanderweyeri*
7 *Synodontis afrofischeri*
8 *Synodontis alberti*

Aquarium size 90×38×30cm (36×15×12in)

Above left: *These illustrations feature typical community systems of Asian species, including suitable catfishes. Be sure to balance such a community so that the upper swimming fishes complement the catfishes. Buying the fishes as youngsters would make it possible to increase the numbers, providing a larger aquarium is available to house the fishes as they mature.*

Above right: *These aquariums represent equivalent community systems based on African species. Provide additional aquascaping in the larger system, including plant pots and rocky caves, because the Synodontis catfishes will compete for the same space as the Kribensis.*

Left: *A Synodontis multipunctatus bent on predation is chased away from Lamprologus brichardi fry by the parent fishes. Keeping cichlids and catfishes together could reduce the numbers of cichlid fry raised but adds to the interest of a community.*

Water requirements and filtration

Since the majority of African and Asian catfishes available for home aquariums are collected directly from the wild, it is important to know something about the natural water conditions in which they live.

African species divide into riverine and lake populations, with a clear contrast in water conditions between the two. Asian species are almost totally found in rivers. The large African rivers – such as the Niger, Nile and Zaire – are typical of the world's major tropical waterways. They begin as relatively small but fast-moving water flows, increasing in volume as various tributaries join forces with them, and as they near the sea they slow down and widen out into the familiar deltas. Different species have become adapted to live in these three distinct zones.

Fast-flowing waters

In Africa, *Chiloglanis* and *Euchilichthys* are the masters of the fast-water flows, flourishing even when the rivers become torrential during the rainy season. In Asia, the

equivalent species are the members of the Sisoridae Family, *Glyptothorax* and *Bagarius* sp. These catfishes have sucker-like, disc-shaped mouths and modified pectoral and ventral fins that enable them to keep a firm grip among boulders and rocks as the water flows past them.

Fast-flowing waters are typically rich in oxygen, relatively cool and have a high pH value (i.e. they are alkaline). Simulating these conditions in the aquarium means providing a strong water flow with internal and external power pumps

Below: *Simulating the fast-flowing waters in which some African and Asian catfishes thrive is possible in the aquarium using suitably placed powerheads. Rocks and sturdy plants complete the environment.*

Above: *This river in Thailand is typical of the slower moving waters that support many of the Asian catfishes available to fishkeepers.*

to keep the water fresh and well aerated. A temperature of 24°C (75°F), a pH value of 7.5 and a general hardness level of 5-10°dH would be ideal.

The middle reaches

In the middle reaches rivers 'put on weight' and their youthful energy gives way to a less hectic flow. Here, topsoil and general forest debris accumulate in the water and tend to lower the pH value to between 5.9 and 6.8 (i.e. from very acidic to slightly acidic). Since the water is moving more slowly, it warms up in the sunshine to reach a temperature range of 25-31°C (77-88°F), depending on season. The hardness of the water is often 0°dH.

In Africa, such middle reaches are home to many species of *Synodontis* plus a host of Bagrids such as *Auchenoglanis* sp., *Chrysichthys* sp. and *Clarotes* sp. In Asia, almost all species available to aquarists live in these waters.

River deltas

The final stages of many big rivers are tidal and the mixture of salt and trace elements that build up in the water tend to raise the pH from

acidic to slightly alkaline values. In Asia, several species of *Mystus* live in deltas or tidal waters and their high salt tolerance makes them ideal subjects for brackish water aquariums. To accommodate catfishes from these waters, provide a fresh, well-aerated system with a pH value of 7.0-7.5, a hardness of 5-15°dH and a temperature of about 25°C (77°F).

African Rift Valley Lakes

The African Rift Valley Lakes provide a completely different environment for catfishes, both in terms of water conditions and general habitat. Lake Malawi and Lake Tanganyika are virtual freshwater seas. Lake Tanganyika is exceptional in that it is 580km (360 miles) long and 1470m (4822ft) deep, second only in depth to Lake Baikal in Russia. The high level of calcium in the Rift Valley Lakes gives the water a pH value of 7.5-8.8, i.e. alkaline. The water temperature remains more or less constant at about 22°C (72°F), although in the shoreline shallows it ranges between 25-29°C (77-84°F).

The value of filtration

In their natural habitats, the majority of catfishes live a benthic, or bottom-dwelling, existence. Therefore, in aquariums they are most likely to remain on the aquarium substrate. Because they are living close to the gravel, or filterbed, any extremes of water quality can lead to health problems in catfishes. A large community of healthy, well-fed fishes produce waste products that must be removed or broken down into harmless compounds. In nature, fishes live in a huge ecosystem in which waste products are quickly diluted and converted into less toxic substances by the natural process of nitrification. (Nitrification is a vital part of the natural 'nitrogen cycle', in which bacteria convert toxic ammonium waste products into nitrites and then to less harmful nitrates.) These physical and biological processes rely on the continuous supply of oxygen to the

system. In ideal natural conditions, moving water open to the air, wind and rain will not contain trapped gases or harbour harmful pollutants. In complete contrast, however, the aquarium is an enclosed system in which wastes are trapped and can rapidly build up into poisons.

In an aquarium, therefore, adequate filtration and aeration are vital parts of the life support system that simulates the fishes' natural environment. Sadly, some fishkeepers spend a greater amount of their aquarium budget on decoration than on the essential requirements of keeping the water clean and healthy. To do so is a

Above: This head detail of Clarias batrachus *shows the prominent barbels that are used to probe the substrate for food particles.*

serious error; the well-being of the fishes depends upon the fishkeeper providing water of consistently good quality in the aquarium.

Filtration for catfishes
It is doubtful if any catfish aquarium would be complete without efficient undergravel filtration of the constant velocity type. Without such substrate filtration, gravel or any other aquarium floor covering is liable to stagnate. When this happens, bacterial infections are likely to spread among bottom-dwelling fishes. A common access for infection in catfishes is through the sensitive barbels should they become physically damaged. Once these sensory extensions become

Below: Combining undergravel and power filtration is very effective in an aquarium containing catfishes. Each works independently and together they prevent harmful substrate and water stagnation.

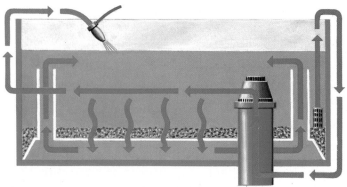

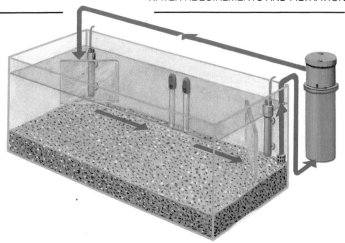

infected, the demise of the fish is predictable. Catfishes *are* hardy, but this simple problem can have fatal results.

Be sure to use at least 7.5cm (3in) of rounded gravel over the filter plates. A particle size of 5mm (3/16in) is ideal. Place rocks and bogwood around the undergravel uplift pipes to prevent them from being displaced by larger catfishes.

The uplifts can be operated by air pumps or power heads. Fitting power heads (electrically driven water pumps) to the tops of the uplift tubes will speed the flow of water through the undergravel filter. Some power heads aerate the water only if they are positioned close to the water surface, so cut down the uplift tubes if necessary to produce this beneficial aeration.

With regular maintenance, undergravel filtration can be used on its own with small to medium-sized systems, from 60x38x30cm (24x15x12in) to 90x38x30cm (36x15x12in), to provide water of a consistently high quality for most community catfishes. Even larger systems, 120x45x30cm to 120x45x38cm (48x18x12in to 48x18x15in), if not excessively stocked, can be operated on a well-maintained undergravel filtration.

Using power filters
For the perfect catfish system, the combination of undergravel and external power filtration is well

Above: Glass partitions siliconed into the corners can provide ideal compartments to conceal heater-thermostats. Allow adequate space top and bottom and place the inlet tube to the power filter in one corner and the outlet tube into the opposite corner. This ensures a constant flow past the heaters.

proved among experienced fishkeepers. The external filter extracts sediment and waste from the water before it can be drawn down into the gravel. Power filters provide a back-up to the nitrifying process by housing beneficial bacteria. In order to provide additional and reliable nitrification over a long period, load power filters with long-term filter media. The alternatives of filter carbon and sponge medium will both support nitrifying bacteria but need more frequent changing. Sponge medium tends to slime up too quickly, while filter carbon has such an unpredictable lifespan before it leaches organic waste products back into the water that it cannot be relied upon.

Ideally, layer the inlet/base area of the power filter with a nylon scourer and some ceramic hollow pots. This will allow water to pass through virtually unimpeded but will trap larger particles and organic debris. Fill the upper part of the filter canister with porous gravel as used in the aquarium. This will provide a

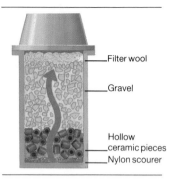

Filter wool

Gravel

Hollow
ceramic pieces

Nylon scourer

Above: *Power filters operate more efficiently if the canister is layered with the correct filter materials, progressing from a coarse to a fine texture as shown here.*

physical and biological filter once bacteria become established on the surface of the gravel particles. Finally, the top 5-7.5cm (2-3in) layer should be filter wool to extract fine particles of sediment from the water as it leaves the filter.

If the aquarium contains large catfishes, reduce the amount of gravel substrate and increase the proportion of ceramic pots in the filter body. And, if necessary, increase the water flow by using a coarser gravel.

Most power filters have venturi adaptors to allow air to bleed into the water flow and this enhances the level of oxygen in the water.

When installing a power filter for the first time on a system, always 'seed' the nitrification process by including some mature gravel or filter medium (i.e. used in an aquarium over 8-10 weeks old) to the new medium. A good aquarium dealer will help you with this if you cannot provide suitable material from an existing aquarium.

Size of power filters

The correct size of power filter for any particular aquarium is not based on applying a rigid formula. It is always best to buy the largest filter you can afford. It is impossible to over-filter aquarium water; clean water is as important to fishes as clean air is to humans.

A power filter should be capable of turning over the aquarium volume two to three times per hour *under pressure*. Manufacturers tend to quote turnover figures for their filters based on an unloaded canister tested under favourable laboratory conditions. In aquariums, once sediment is drawn into the filter medium, the flow rate will fall drastically. Always allow for this.

Below: *A typical external power filter. The removable container allows different filter materials to be used for various water treatment purposes. Correct layering is vital.*

Above: *Remove organic waste from the substrate during water changes using a siphonic device. This will protect catfishes from stagnation.*

If your budget cannot stretch to a power filter when you set up the aquarium, then all is not lost. An undergravel filter (once it has established the bacterial colony) can cope with a new aquarium system for 8 to 12 weeks. To spread the costs, you can add a power filter at this stage without causing undue harm to your fishes.

Maintaining filtration systems
Regular maintenance is one of the most important tasks for the conscientious fishkeeper and is especially vital for filtration systems.

The most important aspect of maintaining good undergravel filtration is to remove the organic sediment from the fishes and plants that builds up in the enclosed environment of the aquarium.

Clean the substrate by using one of the inexpensive syphonic action devices to draw up debris from the gravel particles. Cleaning the gravel in this way every three or four weeks will prevent accumulating dirt from disturbing the pH balance of the water (usually towards unacceptably acidic levels) and ensure the free pasage of oxygen so essential for the nitrifying bacteria to

flourish. It is the equivalent of a gardener turning over the soil.

Cleaning power filters is also a regular but less frequent task. Power filters should be left running until the flow rate is clearly reduced by 60-70 percent. This indicates a significant build up of sediment inside the canister. To clean the filter, empty all the contents into a bucket of water taken from the aquarium. Rinse the medium and filter wool thoroughly in the tank water and return them to the canister. The important point here is the use of aquarium water to clean the filter contents. Avoid the temptation to wash the filter medium under running tapwater; the chlorine in the water can suppress the bacterial activity established in the filter. Rinsing the medium in aquarium water of the correct pH and temperature does not disturb this activity.

Although undergravel and power filtration make an ideal combination, it is possible to use either in isolation. In this case, however, you must be even more meticulous in your maintenance routine. For aquariums operating purely on undergravel filtration, be sure to use gravel cleaners during weekly or fortnightly partial water changes. If you aim to operate an aquarium solely on power filtration, ensure that you use extremely powerful canister filters and that the substrate in the aquarium is shallow. A light scattering of river sand or a shallow pebble layer would be ideal, but you will need to rake this through at least once a week.

Since aquascapes for catfishes feature plenty of rocks and wood, which will impede the flow of water through the substrate, you should seriously consider using both types of filtration in any elaborate aquarium.

Even in the most sophisticated filtration systems, aquariums without good undergravel filtration will be a poorer environment for bottom-dwelling catfishes. A sure sign of substrate stagnation is the hovering activity of catfishes away from the surface of the gravel.

Lighting and heating

Lighting a catfish aquarium requires considerable thought because the majority of species live a nocturnal existence. During the daytime, when they are mostly inactive, catfishes will hide away in the shadows and will appreciate a fairly low light level in the aquarium. This does not mean the lighting should be unadventurous, however. From the onlooker's point of view, an imaginative lighting system can enhance an aquarium; bad lighting can produce a very dull result.

Lighting for catfishes

Fluorescent tubes are widely used for aquarium lighting. They are cheap to run and cool in use, but they direct an even strip of light into the aquarium that produces a predictable effect. The alternative is to use tungsten spotlighting. This can create dramatic effects but has a number of disadvantages. The main objection to spotlighting – and probably the reason why it is so little used – is the difficulty of accommodating the lamp fittings into a narrow aquarium canopy.

Which system of lighting should you use in an aquarium containing African and Asian catfishes? Using a combination of fluorescent tubes and tungsten spotlamps is an ideal choice. Such combinations usually include fluorescent tubes that produce a balanced light output for encouraging plants to grow in aquarium conditions. Since plant growth is often a secondary consideration in catfish systems, why not use spotlamps to achieve dramatic light and shade effects?

The best way to overcome the problems posed by the canopy is to dispense with the canopy altogether and mount spotlights above an open aquarium. Since the top of the tank invariably looks untidy, mount the aquarium a little higher than usual so that the top is not in view. You can then suspend the spotlights in attractive fittings or conceal them behind a facade. Once installed, spotlights directed at a rippling water surface will produce a striking display of angled shafts of light. Catfishes will naturally hide away from these lighted areas but should show some interesting activity in the shadows.

Whatever type of lighting you use, be sure to keep the aquarium regularly maintained so that the lighting is used to its maximum effect. An excess of tannic acid in the water – leaching from unsoaked bogwood, for example – will cause a yellow-brown cast that severely reduces the penetration of light. Efficient filtration and regular partial water changes should prevent any major discoloration of the water. It is also vital to keep the cover glass clean to allow as much light as possible to reach the aquarium.

Heating

Catfishes exist in a wide range of water conditions. Some inhabitants of high mountain streams, such as African *Chiloglanis* and Asian *Glyptothorax* sp., live in a fairly low temperature range of 15-24°C (59-75°F). Others, such as African and Asian *Clarias* sp., can survive the high temperatures found in isolated creeks that recede in the dry season and begin to gain heat and lose oxygen in the process. This shallow water can be 35°C (95°F) in the open and 30°C (86°F) in the shaded areas. Based on these examples, an average temperature range of 24-27°C (75-81°F) will be acceptable to the majority of species available to fishkeepers.

While some aquarium books offer a guide to the wattages required by specific volumes of water, the effect of ambient room temperatures and the failure of heater-thermostat manufacturers to develop a reliable 300-watt model, for example, makes a mockery of rigid rules.

Another factor rarely mentioned in literature is that in an aquarium measuring 60x38x30cm (24x15x12in), for example, a 150-watt heater may be recommended yet a 200-watt heater would be more efficient, using less energy to achieve the desired temperature. Good water circulation in aquarium systems – provided by power heads and more efficient air pumps – aids the distribution of heat.

The table of recommended heating systems shown on this page is a guide based on practical experience of systems in heated rooms during the winter, when the ambient temperatures are usually 24°C (75°F) or more. If the room has long periods during which it is unheated, increase the wattage by 50 percent to help combat the likely fluctuations in air temperatures that will in turn affect the aquarium.

Since catfishes are often burned by resting against a heater element, it is essential to shield the unit. Some fishkeepers have succeeded in combating this problem by wrapping a strip of gravel tidy (plastic mesh) loosely around the element and fixed with a cable tie.

Some catfishes, *Clarias* for example, grow quite large and are extremely destructive towards heaters and aquarium filter plate uplifts. If a power filter is used in conjunction with good constant velocity undergravel filters, then it is possible to position heater-thermostats and power filter inlet and outlet tubes in corner compartments away from the attentions of inquisitive catfishes, as shown on page 19.

As an alternative to standard heater-thermostats, consider using a thermofilter – basically a large power filter with a heater element within the canister head. Or invest in an 'all-in-one' aquarium system in which the pumps, filtration and heating equipment is housed in a separate compartment as part of a reverse-flow filter set-up.

Above: *Combining different types of lighting can be the key to success in the catfish aquarium. Spotlighting can create contrasts of light and dark that mirror habitat conditions.*

Below: *The heater ratings given here are slightly higher than normally suggested to provide a safety margin and efficient use of energy in maintaining temperatures.*

Recommended heating systems

Aquarium size (L×D×W)

60×38×30 cm (24×15×12 in)
1×200 watt heater-thermostat

60×45×30 cm (24×18×12 in)
1×200 watt heater-thermostat

90×38×30 cm (36×15×12 in)
1×200 watt heater-thermostat

90×45×38 cm (36×18×15 in)
1×150 watt + 1×100 watt heater-thermostats

120×38×30 cm (48×15×12 in)
1×200 watt + 1×100 watt heater-thermostats

120×45×38 cm (48×18×15 in)
1×200 watt + 1×150 watt heater-thermostats

150×45×38 cm (60×18×15 in)
3×200 watt heater-thermostats

180×45×45 cm (72×18×18 in)
4×200 watt heater-thermostats

Aquascaping

An aquarium layout for catfishes should provide plenty of daytime hiding places for these largely nocturnal fishes. It is unusual to set up a catfish-only aquarium, however, precisely because of the lack of daytime (and therefore watchable) activity. The more likely inclusion of catfishes in tanks with other types of fishes calls for a compromise aquascape that will suit all the inhabitants. A particularly interesting example concerns the African Rift Lake species of *Synodontis*, which enjoy a special relationship with mouthbrooding cichlids. (For more details, see page 37.) In aquariums, this has led to successful spawnings of *Synodontis multipunctatus* from Lake Tanganyika in which eggs produced by the catfishes are raised 'cuckoo style' by mouthbrooding cichlids. In such a Rift Lake aquascape, the same layout of rocks and caves will suit both catfishes and cichlids admirably.

An Asian aquascape should recreate an acidic riverway or creek with a substrate littered with large rounded pebbles and driftwood debris. Use power head pumps to create a water flow across the substrate to simulate the river conditions. Catfishes of the genus *Mystus*, *Leiocassis*, *Chaca*, *Kryptopterus* and *Bagarius* would thrive in such a system. Creating a river banking effect by using bogwood pieces would allow these fishes to hide and yet remain in view of the fishkeeper. This system would also suit a community of riverine *Synodontis*, although these catfishes are less free swimming than the Asian forms listed above and as such would require extra caves and branches to provide shade and hiding places in the aquarium.

For larger disruptive catfishes, such as the Asian and African *Clarias* or the African species *Auchenoglanis*, any delicate aquascape would be bulldozed away in moments. A robust system of rocks and bogwood is necessary for these fishes, although a cave in which a territory can be occupied is still a priority for them.

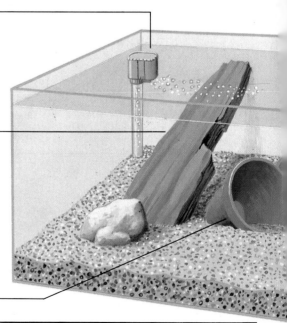

Use a powerhead on the uplift from the undergravel filter to speed filtration rate and set up water currents across the aquarium.

Large pieces of slate can replace the more familiar bogwood in this aquascape to create shade and hiding places for the catfishes.

Plant pots make excellent 'caves' for the fishes to find refuge from light and from the attentions of other catfishes.

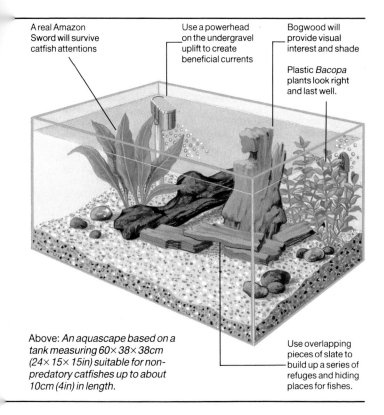

A real Amazon Sword will survive catfish attentions

Use a powerhead on the undergravel uplift to create beneficial currents

Bogwood will provide visual interest and shade

Plastic *Bacopa* plants look right and last well.

Above: *An aquascape based on a tank measuring 60×38×38cm (24×15×15in) suitable for non-predatory catfishes up to about 10cm (4in) in length.*

Use overlapping pieces of slate to build up a series of refuges and hiding places for fishes.

Below: *This rocky unplanted aquascape in a 90×38×38cm* (36×15×15in) tank is ideal for Rift Lake Synodontis catfishes.

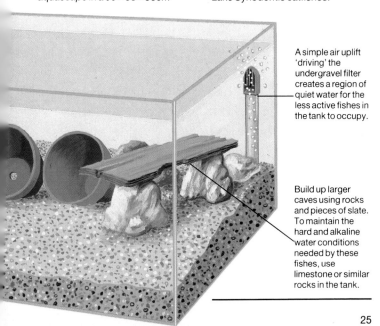

A simple air uplift 'driving' the undergravel filter creates a region of quiet water for the less active fishes in the tank to occupy.

Build up larger caves using rocks and pieces of slate. To maintain the hard and alkaline water conditions needed by these fishes, use limestone or similar rocks in the tank.

Some fishkeepers use large drainage pipes in a catfish aquarium to provide hiding places for the fishes. This is not ideal, however, since the fishes cannot be seen by the fishkeeper, and several catfishes disputing over the same pipe can cause a great deal of damage as they jostle for position. An alternative approach is to use twisted beech branches, which can be taken dead from the tree, debarked and soaked. A substantial and intricately formed piece will provide plenty of catfish hideaways. Because light penetrates from above, each fish will feel secure resting in the shade beneath a branch. The fishes can still be viewed from the front of the tank, so one of the priorities of fishkeeping is taken care of. If large beechwood branches are not available, use long strips of bogwood laid out in a similar fashion.

Planting

The major requirement of any plant used in an aquarium containing catfishes is that it should be robust. Larger catfishes are not averse to turning over the substrate in search of food and in doing so will undoubtedly disturb plant roots. The night-time activity of catfishes involves a considerable amount of bumping into obstacles. Very few catfishes have well-developed eyes – since they would be useless in darkness – and therefore most catfishes use their sensory barbels to guide them. And, of course, the subdued lighting levels ideal for catfishes are hardly conducive to good plant growth.

Artificial plants certainly solve the problem in a positive way, but combining living plants with plastic replicas is perhaps the ideal solution. Whereas real specimens of soft-leaved plants such as *Cardamine*, *Luwigia* and *Bacopa* would not withstand the blundering manoeuvres of a foraging catfish, their plastic counterparts will look more than presentable in the aquarium. They can be combined with living specimens of large

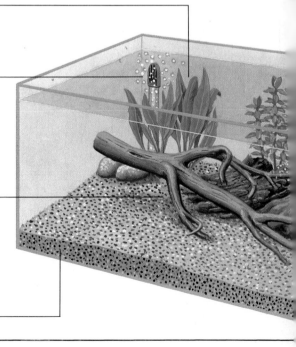

Real Amazon Swords can thrive at the low light levels catfishes prefer.

Use air uplifts in the corners of the tank and suitable powerheads in the centre. There are four filter plates beneath the gravel, each fitted widthways.

In such a long tank, a twisted beech branch can be used as the centrepiece of the aquascape design. It provides both shade and refuges.

Use rounded gravel of 5mm (³/₁₆in) particle size, at least 7.5cm (3in) deep over the undergravel filter.

Above: *Since most real plants will not thrive in the low lighting conditions preferred by catfishes, plastic plants are ideal for creating a natural-looking effect.*

Amazon Swords,(*Echinodorus sp.*) *Cryptocorynes*, and Java Fern (*Microsorium pteropus*), which will survive lower light levels and the physical clumsiness of catfishes.

When using plastic plants, try to create the illusion of growth by buying several sizes of the same plant and arranging them in a group. The effect will be of the plant at various stages of development.

Because undergravel filtration is much maligned by plant experts, who argue that the water flow through the gravel affects root growth, set the roots of real plants in small trays of growing medium buried in the gravel. The trays used to hold fresh vegetables in supermarkets are ideal for plants.

Direct the flow from one powerhead forwards and the other along the back of the tank.

Below: *This 120× 45×38cm (48× 18× 15in) tank plays host to an aquascape designed for predatory catfishes up to about 25cm (10in).*

Using a plastic version of a plant such as *Bacopa* creates a delicate realistic effect.

Protect the base of the air uplifts with pebbles. This will safeguard them against the digging actions of the catfishes.

Slate and rounded boulders make perfect caves and hiding places for catfishes. Ensure that any such constructions are stable; they can easily damage the tank glass should they collapse.

Feeding and routine maintenance

In terms of their natural diet, and – more importantly – how they obtain it, African and Asian catfishes can be divided into two major types: scavengers and predators. In this section we briefly review the natural eating habits of catfishes and how to feed them successfully in the aquarium. Then we look at routine maintenance tasks in the aquarium.

Scavenging catfishes

Many small to medium-sized catfishes in the genera *Chiloglanis*, *Kryptopterus*, *Mochokiella* and *Synodontis* could be termed 'sifter' scavengers because they tend to root into the substrate for food. In their natural habitat, these catfishes eat algae, small shrimps, snails, fly larvae and general silt debris. It is easy to reproduce this broad diet in the aquarium by providing normal dried flake food, freeze-dried *Tubifex*, mosquito larvae and bloodworm, plus tablet food. Use frozen foods to make up the invertebrate part of the diet in the form of Gamma shrimp, prawn, and brineshrimp.

Live foods in the form of *Daphnia*, bloodworms and *Tubifex* are ideal for bringing fishes into spawning condition, although there is a risk of introducing diseases into the aquarium. Using frozen packets of these foods removes the risk of spreading infections and also prevents the accidental introduction of parasites and snails.

Predatory catfishes

Catfishes in the genera *Bagarius*, *Chaca*, *Chrysichthys*, *Clarias*, *Clarotes*, *Leiocassis*, *Mystus*, *Pangasius*, and *Wallago* are more or less predatory, being fast swimmers that prowl in the darkness for small fishes. (Interesting exceptions are the *Auchenoglanis* species, which grow large but tend to remain sifters rather than killers.) In their natural environment, these catfishes consume small fishes, large freshwater/brackish shrimps and crabs, large aquatic insects and drowned land animals.

In recent years, food manufacturers have developed new products for feeding such large fishes. Notable among these are foodsticks – literally worm-like sticks of food that provide a welcome break from the traditional flaked foods. Some flake foods are produced in large flake sizes and pellet foods are also widely available. Frozen foods can reproduce the needs of large fishes in the form of whole shrimp, krill, lancefish and whole cockle. Live food (excluding fishes) can be offered in the form of large earthworms, slugs, beetles and lice.

Rift Valley Lake *Synodontis* require a high proportion of crustaceans in the diet to duplicate their natural food source. Riverine fishes are not so specialized and tend to be more opportunistic feeders. Ensure that the food is small enough or at least easy for them to break down.

Large predatory *Mystus* from Asia or *Bagrus* from Africa require large food, such as whole shrimp, whole prawns, whitebait and large earthworms to sustain them.

Feed large fishes on alternate days. This not only allows them time to digest food but also eases pressure on the filtration system within the enclosed environment of the aquarium. This feeding pattern will suit predatory fishes, since they do not always encounter food on a daily basis in the wild and will sometimes fast for long periods. Large fishes typically have empty stomachs when they are spawning or migrating during high water seasons. Most large adult aquarium fishes could remain without food for 7 to 14 days and not come to any harm. In such a period, the fishes rely on stored body fat and, although some disturbance would develop between individuals in a community system because of hunger, permanent damage is unlikely to occur.

The final word on feeding catfishes has to be a stress on the need for variety. It is important to offer a range of foods of suitable size in order to keep catfishes successfully for long periods. The charts offer some suggestions.

FEEDING CHART
Small to medium-sized, non-predatory catfishes

Species	Suitable foods (Percentage over a weekly period)	Feeding frequency
Chiloglanis cameronensis Euchilichthys guentheri Eutropiellus vanderweyeri Hemisynodontis membranaceus Kryptopterus bicirrhis Mochokiella paynei Most Synodontis species	Bloodworm, gnat larvae 35 percent Flake food 25 percent Shrimps, prawns, brineshrimp, cockle, mussel 10 percent Tablet food 10 percent Whiteworm, chopped earthworms, crushed beetles 10 percent Food sticks 5 percent Lettuce/Spinach 5 percent	A combination of any food twice daily

FEEDING CHART
Predatory catfishes

Species	Suitable foods (Percentage over a weekly period)	Feeding frequency
Bagarius bagarius Chaca chaca Chrysichthys ornatus Clarias batrachus Clarotes laticeps Leiocassis siamensis Leiocassis stenomus Malapterurus electricus Mystus species Pangasius sutchi Wallago attu	Prawn, shrimp, small crabs, cockle, mussel 50 percent Earthworms, maggots, beetles, slugs, etc. 25 percent Foodsticks or pellets 15 percent Fish 10 percent	Feed every other day

FEEDING CHART
African Rift Valley Lake *Synodontis* species

Species	Suitable foods (Percentage over a weekly period)	Feeding frequency
Synodontis dhonti *eurystomus* *multipunctatus* *njassae* *petricolor*	Chopped mussel and cockle, shrimp, brineshrimp, Gamma shrimp, shredded prawns 50 percent	A combination of any food twice daily
	Mosquito larvae, gnat larvae 25 percent	
	Flake (including green flake), plus spinach 25 percent	

Maintenance

The routine tasks necessary to maintain an aquarium containing catfishes are those recommended for all community systems. Here we review the basic jobs involved.

Water changes and pH

Most aquarists are aware that partial water changes help to keep the system healthy by improving water quality and controlling pH balance, but do not realize the need to extract sediment from the substrate on a regular basis. It can be proved that in a low pH situation (i.e. one in which the aquarium water is becoming undesirably acidic) simply making a partial water change of up to 50 percent will not have any lasting effect on the pH value in the aquarium. By contrast, making a 30 percent water change and removing accumulated silt from the substrate with a siphonic cleaning device, plus the addition of a pH corrector such as sodium carbonate, will lift the pH to a satisfactory level. Of course, the results will vary according to the pH levels in question, both of the aquarium water and the local tapwater, but the general principle holds true for most situations.

If the water supply is slightly acidic *and* very soft, preventing an imbalance of pH in the aquarium will involve adding calcium and magnesium. The best way to do this is to add crushed cockleshells or crushed coral to the substrate. This will increase the water hardness and raise the pH value of the water at the same time. The amounts required will depend on the water supply.

It is not widely known that the pH value of water in an aquarium is influenced by the substrate, the amount of organic debris in the water, the stocking levels and the domestic supply. More fish and therefore more waste and excess protein in the system can reduce the oxygen exchange at the water surface. As the carbon dioxide levels increase, the fishes increase their gill rates to extract more oxygen from the water – a sure sign of distress. Aquarium fishes thrive in water that is 'fresh', full of oxygen and clean for them to 'breathe' in. As a visual test of water quality, check to see if bubbles are clustering at the water surface. If they are, this is a sign that excess protein is polluting the system. Draw off a glass of tank water and stand it on a white card. If it is yellowish, carry out a partial water change and extract sediment from the substrate at the same time.

Weekly checks

On a weekly basis check the power filter or power head flow for strength. If the external power filter flow has slowed down significantly then clean out the canister as described in the filtration section on page 21. A reduced flow on a power head signals a blockage in the undergravel system and the time may have arrived to withdraw sediment from the gravel.

Every week check the pH value and temperature of the water; the latter can vary if room temperatures are extreme. If airstones are employed in undergravel filter uplifts, check these regularly. A reduction in aeration usually signifies the failure of an airstone. These accessories are cheap to replace and, if left on the filtration system in a blocked condition, they can reduce the efficiency of both the undergravel filtration and pump. A blocked airstone can put unnecessary back pressure on the air pump and this in turn will shorten the life of valves and diaphragms.

During the first few weeks of an aquarium's life, be sure to test the water regularly for nitrite level. As the system matures – in a bacterial sense – nitrite levels will peak within three to five weeks and then gradually fall as the level of nitrates increases. Once such a peak has occurred in a new system, it rarely recurs. If the nitrite level remains high in an established system, this may indicate a breakdown in the biological filtration system. In this case, seek further advice from your local aquatic dealer, who will know your particular set-up in detail.

General maintenance

General maintenance to the aquarium will arise at different times. In addition to replacing failed components, it usually involves keeping the system clean. In this respect, cleaning away algae as it develops may occupy a large proportion of the time spent on general maintenance.

Clean algae from the front glass by using a pan scourer, but not the type impregnated with soap or other

Above: *A certain amount of green algae can be beneficial, but control filamentous forms such as these.*

cleaning agent. Cover glasses also become covered in a film of algae; the brightly lit, moist environment just beneath the tank lights offers an ideal opportunity for these plant cells to proliferate. Cleaning glass/plastic condensation covers regularly eases the task; algae left to build up over a long period can be very difficult to remove.

A certain amount of algae covering the rocks in the aquarium can be considered natural. The cells absorb nitrates in the water as fertilizer and the large surface area of the algal mass harbours beneficial bacteria that assist in the natural cycle of nitrification. In this way, algae can help to balance the aquarium.

Excess algal growths – often filamentous algae – can be unattractive and damaging to the aquarium system. Such rampant algal growth can be caused by too high a level of nitrates and other compounds that plants use as fertilizers. Usually, however, it indicates that the lighting is too strong or has been left on too long. Sunlight striking directly into the tank – although creating a pleasing effect and not to be avoided totally – can cause 'algal blooms' very rapidly because the light is so 'spectrally rich'. If algae caused by sunlight builds up across the substrate and the glass, move the tank or shade it from the sun to control the problem.

Basic health care

Catfishes and diseases are not normally associated with each other. Fishkeepers generally consider catfishes to be tough, hardy and capable of withstanding the worst that nature and aquariums can produce. An extension of this line of thought is the naive illusion that once a catfish is introduced into an aquarium all maintenance will become unnecessary.

In reality, such thinking results in hardy fishes being abused and falling foul of extreme infections. When diseases strike a strong animal the results are usually fatal, largely because it is so difficult to recognize the symptoms and provide the correct treatment in good time. Of course, it is never enough simply to treat the problem without identifying and correcting the underlying cause. This is as true for catfishes – although admittedly tougher than most – as it is for all aquarium fishes.

Experience shows that established fishes develop infections because of three basic causes:

1 Incorrect diet
2 Unstable water conditions (such as falling pH level) resulting from equipment failure/poor filtration
3 The introduction of infected fishes into a healthy set-up

As far as catfishes are concerned, a high percentage of infections can be linked with water stagnation, which originates in the lower stratum of the aquarium – their domain. Once the water quality has been improved, simple bacterial infections, such as fin rot, can be treated reasonably easily by adding one of the proprietary antibacterial remedies directly to the aquarium water.

Not all fin and body damage is caused by disease, however. Such damage may result from overcrowding and/or the lack of a suitable aquascape for the fishes concerned. Because most catfishes are nocturnal, it can be difficult to detect damage and disease before it is too late to take appropriate action or apply a treatment.

If catfishes show signs of parasite infestation, the same underlying 'environmental' causes may be responsible as those listed for diseases. Again, many broad-range anti-parasite treatments are available, but finding the root cause is vital to avoid further problems.

Once the cause has been identified and corrected, the treatment administered to the fishes must be given time to work; overnight improvements are rare. Parasite infestations may not come to light until they have reached an advanced stage, in which case the treatment constantly struggles to catch up and overtake the condition. One such example is a velvet-like complaint that appears almost to asphyxiate affected fishes before treatment begins to take effect. This particular killer condition begins with similar symptoms to

Below: *This* Mochokiella paynei *has a swollen belly, a condition that may be caused by incorrect feeding, substrate stagnation or an infection.*

those of white spot (ich), but eventually spreads over the body in a dust-like covering. (Velvet and white spot are both caused by unicellular parasites.) This infection is typical of the contagious conditions that can be introduced through unquarantined stock.

The table shows the health problems that may afflict catfishes, their likely causes and possible treatments. If the water quality is good and the feeding regime is suitable, however, most fishes will

Below: *Fin and body damage, seen on this* Synodontis brichardi, *will respond to antibacterial cures, correct diet and good water quality.*

Above: *The fine 'pepper' white spot seen on this* Synodontis *catfish requires suitable treatment over a long period. It is caused by extreme imbalances in water conditions.*

overcome normal infections. In the artifically enclosed system of an aquarium, the environment must be wholesome; otherwise disease and parasitic infestations will take hold.

Stocking levels are also important. The close contact of fishes within an overcrowded aquarium is a devastatingly effective way of spreading diseases quickly. In understocked aquariums – a rare state of affairs – disease is less likely to dominate.

TABLE OF HEALTH PROBLEMS

Signs of infection or abnormal behaviour	Possible causes	Action
Fishes gasping at the water surface	Excess ammonia/ nitrate levels in a new aquarium	Carry out a partial water change and seed filter bed with mature gravel
	Incorrect pH, poor water quality, stagnant substrate, inadequate filtration	Carry out a partial water change and remove sediment from gravel. Check pH and add a pH corrector if necessary. Check filter and pump size to see if they are capable of coping with the system
Fishes hanging in midwater in a vertical position	Excess ammonia/ nitrite levels in a new aquarium	Carry out a partial water change and seed filter bed with mature gravel
	Incorrect pH, poor water quality, stagnant substrate, inadequate filtration	Carry out a partial water change and remove sediment from gravel. Check pH and add a pH corrector if necessary. Check filter and pump size to see if they are capable of coping with the system
	Water poisoned with insect spray, cleaning agents, etc.	Carry out a 100 percent water change. Use dechlorinating chemicals to avoid damage to filter beds
	White spot (Ich) (Ichthyophthirius multifiliis) Freshwater velvet (Oodinium pillularis)	Use a proprietary white spot or velvet treatment as directed by maker
Fishes flicking, itching and scraping body against gravel, wood or rockwork	Excess ammonia/ nitrite levels in a new aquarium	Carry out a partial water change and seed filter bed with mature gravel
	Incorrect pH, poor water quality, stagnant substrate, inadequate filtration	Carry out a partial water change and remove sediment from gravel. Check pH and add a pH corrector if necessary. Check filter and pump size to see if they are capable of coping with the system

Signs of infection or abnormal behaviour	Possible causes	Action
	White spot (Ich) Freshwater velvet	Use a proprietary white spot or velvet treatment as directed by maker
	Gill flukes (*Dactylogyrus* and other species)	Use a proprietary anti-parasite remedy
Red blotches, gills inflamed	Gill flukes (*Dactylogyrus* etc.)	Use a proprietary anti-parasite remedy
Cloudy eyes, as evidence of bacterial infection	Incorrect pH, poor water quality, stagnant substrate, inadequate filtration	Carry out a partial water change and remove sediment from gravel. Check pH and add a pH corrector if necessary. Check filter and pump size to see if they are capable of coping with the system. Add a general antibacterial treatment or tonic
Weight loss	Incorrect diet	Check and revise feeding strategy
Hollow belly, swollen belly	Incorrect diet	Check and revise feeding strategy
	Stagnant substrate	Carry out a partial water change and remove sediment from the gravel
Bloated body, swollen body	Incorrect diet	Check and revise feeding strategy
	Wasting disease – Fish TB (*Mycobacterium*)	Difficult to treat. Keep fishes in good conditions to bolster their natural resistance
	Incorrect pH, poor water quality, stagnant substrate, inadequate filtration	Carry out a partial water change and remove sediment from gravel. Check pH and add a pH corrector if necessary. Check filter and pump size to see if they are capable of coping with the system
Split fins, body scratches	Overcrowding	Check and revise stocking levels

Breeding

Very few African and Asian catfishes have been spawned in captivity, although scientific research has revealed how certain catfishes breed in the wild, notably *Synodontis* and *Clarias*. Commercial and scientific spawnings of *Clarias* are well documented in literature, but the large size of sexually mature specimens means that they are not relevant to fishkeepers.

Aquarium breeding successes involving African members of the scaleless Family *Bagridae* are relatively recent in fishkeeping terms. *Lophiobagrus*, dwarf catfishes from Lake Tanganyika, appeared to be the first African bagrids to be bred in the aquarium. A pair of *Lophiobagrus cyclurus* dug a pit under a group of rocks and guarded a clutch of twenty eggs or so. At about the same time, reports suggested that *Synodontis multipunctatus*, also from Lake Tanganyika, spawned in cuckoo fashion with cichlids. News of this unique interrelationship caused a great stir among catfish enthusiasts and is still the subject of debate. Very recently, two *Mystus* species have been spawned, with egg production in the hundreds in both cases and many fry raised successfully.

Here, we look in more detail at aquarium breeding in *Synodontis* and *Mystus*.

Breeding in Synodontis

The most collectable group of catfishes to breed are certainly members of the genus *Synodontis*. Even so, these breeding successes revolve principally around very brief accounts of spawning *Synodontis nigriventris*, one of the smallest species, and the unique cuckoo-style breeding reported in *Synodontis multipunctatus*.

The distinct lack of success achieved in breeding *Synodontis* when compared with the South American catfishes, such as *Corydoras*, is notable. This can probably be explained by the original high price of *Synodontis* catfishes, which prevented

aquarists from purchasing a group. Recently, Zaire exports of *Synodontis* have become very frequent, and catfishes in general make up a high percentage of the shipments. This means that since more *Synodontis* are available, the price has fallen accordingly and it would appear that successful spawnings are only 'just around the corner'.

Sexing *Synodontis* is not exactly easy, although females are more robust and adult males generally display a genital extension. If it proves difficult to sex individuals then keep a group of three or more together and raise them to breeding condition.

Leaving the African Rift Valley Lake species aside for a moment, habitat information relating to the river-dwelling species of *Synodontis* suggests that they spawn during the high waters of the rainy season. During the dry season, water temperature increases and food is often scarce, whereas the rains cool the water and flood an abundance of food into the rivers.

This situation can be simulated in the aquarium by running a high temperature in the range 28-30°C (83-86°F) and feeding sparingly over a period of two months. Then making a 50 percent water change with cooler water, and dropping the water temperature by 3-6°C (5-10°F) over two or three days may stimulate a spawning. Alternatively, set up a separate aquarium with cooler water, light aeration from a box filter and subdued lighting. A 'pair' of *Synodontis* placed into such an aquarium could be spawned in the same way as barbs or tetras, i.e. using a base of marbles or spawning mops into which spawning pairs could scatter eggs and be unable to eat all of them. A 560mm (22in) *Synodontis schall*, for example, was recorded as carrying 141,000 eggs, which would require a great deal of aquarium space for fry rearing!

Rift Valley Lake *Synodontis* appear uninhibited by the seasons, although some research suggests that certain species spawn in a

Above: *This small breeding tank is ideal for Asian and African egg-scatterers. A substrate of marbles and rounded pebbles allows the eggs to fall out of reach and prevents the adults eating them.*

sequence of spurts between the rainy seasons. Much of the information relating to the Rift Valley Lake species has been reported in aquarium and commercial collections of *Synodontis multipunctatus*. In Lake Tanganyika this species shoals across the sand floor and rock boulders around the perimeter of the lake.

Several Tanganyikan cichlids have been caught with *Synodontis* fry inside the mouth of the female, notably *Cyphotilapia frontosa*. It was first thought that the fry entered the cichlids' mouths while they slept, the catfishes being more active during the night. Aquarium reports, however, suggest a more bizarre explanation. It appears that these catfishes are opportunists and spawn among the cichlids as they spawn. The catfishes eat some of the cichlid eggs while adding a few of their own at the same time. They then leave the mouthbrooding 'foster parents' the job of rearing their fry. Some records suggest the catfish fry then reduce the number of cichlid offspring held in the mother's mouth.

Fishkeepers wishing to become involved with this fascinating area should install a few specimens of *Synodontis multipunctatus* into a

well-aquascaped cichlid community. The majority of aquarium spawnings have involved Malawi cichlids, such as *Pseudotropheus* sp. Thus, almost any Rift Valley cichlid community could provide the correct environment for breeding success.

Breeding in Mystus
In comparison to the obscure behaviour of certain Rift Valley Lake *Synodontis*, *Mystus armatus* and *Mystus vittatus* have proved prolific spawners in a much more conventional manner. These Asian catfishes scatter huge numbers of eggs indiscriminately across the aquarium, males presumably adding sperm to the water during the spawning runs and embraces. In this situation, where hundreds of eggs are produced, many remain unfertilized. To prevent the infertile eggs from affecting the viable ones, it is advisable to add a general tonic or antifungal treatment to the water.

The parent fishes will eat eggs, but normally such high numbers are produced that the situation will not prevent some fry from developing. Removing the adult fishes from the tank, however, will certainly reduce fry predation and raise the chances of rearing a reasonable brood.

The main keys to successful spawnings are to raise a group of the target species to sexual maturity (75 percent of the attainable size is a good guide), offer a varied diet and provide a balanced aquarium system with a practical aquascape.

Species section

This part of the book looks in detail at a representative selection of species available from Africa and Asia. They are presented in alphabetical order of scientific name, followed by an appropriate common name and headings to summarize habitat, mature size, diet, sexual differences, aquarium compatibility and breeding.

The difference in appearance between juvenile and adult fishes is especially marked in many catfishes. Photographs often show adult specimens in excellent health, whereas the young, freshly imported fishes available at your local dealer are likely to appear quite different. Mature specimens often display fin extensions. *Synodontis decorus* and *S. eupterus* are classic examples of this, with the juveniles having a normal dorsal fin. Colour patterns can also differ dramatically between youngsters and adults. *Synodontis dhonti*, superbly spotted and displaying white-edged fins at 7.5-10cm (3-4in), is a much less attractive plain grey with black pepper-

ing at 30cm (12in). This difference so confounded scientists that they classified the two colour forms as distinct species. A dramatic colour change is seen in *Auchenoglanis occidentalis*, which is delightfully patterned as a juvenile yet a much less engaging plain brown when mature. The Asian Bumblebee Catfish, *Leiocassis siamensis*, is strikingly banded in black and yellowish-white at 2.5-5cm (1-2in) and yet invariably black with faint traces of grey-white bands at a mature 15cm (6in). Stress can also be reflected in body colour and pattern; newly imported fishes are often stressed, showing a 'fright' or pale pattern.

African and Asian catfishes provide all the diversity a keen aquarist desires. They are exciting, unpredictable and almost unknown, even to modern-day scientists. This selection of more than 50 species contains some that are ideal for beginners and others that will present a real challenge to catfish enthusiasts.

Above:
Auchenoglanis occidentalis
An attractively patterned juvenile with the distinctive snout, which it uses to sift the substrate for food.

Auchenoglanis occidentalis
Giraffe-nosed Catfish
- **Habitat:** Rivers and lakes of Africa
- **Length:** 600mm (24in)
- **Diet:** Wide ranging, including shrimp, earthworms and fish
- **Sex differences:** Males are possibly more highly coloured and more slender than females
- **Aquarium compatibility:** Ideally suited to most large-fish communities. Accepts a wide pH range of 6.6-8.1
- **Aquarium breeding:** Not known

Juvenile Giraffe-nosed Catfishes are almost irresistible to fishkeepers with a soft spot for unusual catfishes. In the adults, however, the attractive giraffe blotch pattern pales to a less attractive brownish tone, although when they reach adult size few aquariums could provide enough space to accommodate them. In the wild, these fishes use their long snouts to dig into the river silt for all manner of insect and crustacean foods. In the aquarium, the digging capabilities of large specimens can be extremely disruptive and damaging to filter beds and therefore to the water quality over a period of time.

Obviously, this is not the catfish to introduce to a well-planted, delicately aquascaped system, but when young it is an ideal fish to mix with large cichlids or characins.

Bagarius bagarius
Giant Flatmouth Catfish
- **Habitat:** Fast waters in large Asian rivers, such as the Ganges and Mekong basins.
- **Length:** 200mm (8in)
- **Diet:** Insects
- **Sex differences:** Unknown
- **Aquarium compatibility:** Predatory towards small fishes and therefore unsuitable for community systems
- **Aquarium breeding:** Not known

This unusual catfish is often misidentified as *Glyptothorax*, a smaller flat-mouthed, fast-water catfish. Several species of *Bagarius* are known, including a monster species that grows up to 1.8m (6ft) in length.

Bagarius are notoriously difficult to stabilize in aquariums – a high volume of aeration and a steady pH in the range 7.1-7.5 are required in order to acclimatize these fishes successfully into captivity.

Brachysynodontis batensoda
Giant Upside-down Catfish
- **Habitat:** Widespread in the basins of the Nile, Niger, Volta and Chad Rivers

Above: **Bagarius bagarius**
A half-grown Borneo specimen. The beige and brown pattern camouflages it against the river sand.

- **Length:** 200-250mm (8-10in)
- **Diet:** The gill-filters show this fish to be a plankton feeder. In the aquarium, provide shrimp, insect larvae, chopped earthworms, foodsticks and pellets.
- **Sex differences:** Not obvious, although deeper bodied fishes are possibly female
- **Aquarium compatibility:** Reasonably peaceful among other catfishes. Ideal in a community system of large fishes
- **Aquarium breeding:** Not known

A large inverting species well known to enthusiasts as the emblem of the Catfish Association of Great Britain. It is recognizable through its large adipose fin and cannot be mistaken for *Hemisynodontis* because it lacks the membraned maxillary barbels characteristic of that species. *Brachysynodontis* has proved extremely hardy and adaptable in the aquarium and will thrive in acidic or alkaline systems. Feeding has not proved a problem; once settled they will take almost any food, especially foodsticks, pellets and shrimps.

Below:
Brachysynodontis batensoda
The largest truly inverting catfish.

Above: **Chaca chaca**
Like the true Angler Fish, this predatory catfish attracts its unsuspecting prey by means of worm-like lures, in this case the barbels. A fascinating species.

Chaca chaca
Frogmouth; Angler Catfish
- **Habitat:** Brahmaputra/Ganges drainage basin of India and Bangladesh, in rivers and creeks outside the normal rain forest areas
- **Length:** 180mm (7in)
- **Diet:** Fish and crustaceans
- **Sex differences:** Not known
- **Aquarium compatibility:** Can be kept with large fishes and will eventually feed on prawn pieces, etc. Small specimens will starve unless fed deliberately
- **Aquarium breeding:** Not known

Observations of this nocturnal catfish in its natural habitat make interesting reading. '*Chaca* are inactive most of the time; they rest motionless on the substrate for long periods and when approached by small fish the maxillary barbels are moved in such a way as to be mistaken for a worm – luring its prey. Once an unsuspecting fish is within range, *Chaca* sucks its prey into the oral cavity.' It is the extraordinary *Chaca* mouth that gives away its predatory nature.

Another species, *Chaca bankanensis*, which occurs only in the rain forest creeks of the Southern Malay Peninsula and Indonesia, has a darker colour pattern than *Chaca chaca*.

Below: **Chiloglanis cameronensis**
The African Suckermouth requires a constant supply of fine shrimp and bloodworm in a well-aerated tank. Suitable for medium communities.

rock substrate of clear, swiftly flowing streams, especially in torrential stretches.

The dorsal and pectoral spines are needle sharp and are likely to cause severe pain if accidentally handled. Evidence suggests that *Chiloglanis* produces a fluid or mucus which acts as an irritant or anti-coagulant in the wound.

Few aquariums provide the correct environment for the Suckermouth Catfish – clear, neutral, highly oxygenated water.

Chrysichthys ornatus
Ornate Catfish
- **Habitat:** Zaire River
- **Length:** 200mm (8in)
- **Diet:** Crustaceans, insect larvae and fish fry
- **Sex differences:** Not known
- **Aquarium compatibility:** Small specimens can be kept with medium-sized fishes, but large individuals of 150mm (6in) or more will predate on slow-moving fishes
- **Aquarium breeding:** Not known

Chrysichthys ornatus is relatively rare among Zaire imports, but is usually available in small quantities. Adult specimens tend to have a faded colour pattern, but the juvenile to semi-adult catfishes are boldly banded in brown and black on a gold and silver background.

Chiloglanis cameronensis
African Suckermouth Catfish
- **Habitat:** Fast-flowing African streams
- **Length:** 75mm (3in)
- **Diet:** Insect larvae
- **Sex differences:** Males have longer pectoral spines than females
- **Aquarium compatibility:** Ideally suited to medium-sized community systems
- **Aquarium breeding:** Not known

The flat body and well-developed mouth enable this small catfish to live successfully in and around the

Below: **Chrysichthys ornatus**
Closely related to Clarotes sp., *this is also a fish predator that will adapt to a more civilized diet of shrimp and foodsticks in the aquarium.*

Above: **Clarias batrachus**
The Walking Catfish uses its barbels to probe the substrate for food. Keep large fishes singly.

Clarias batrachus

Walking Catfish
- **Habitat:** Widespread in Asian rivers and pools
- **Length:** 450mm (18in)
- **Diet:** Any food accepted
- **Sex differences:** Adult males have thickened pectoral spines.
- **Aquarium compatibility:** Large specimens can be difficult to keep with large community fishes because they are voracious feeders capable of shredding the fins of less robust species
- **Aquarium breeding:** Commercial and scientific experiments have resulted in many spawnings. A large system is required

This species is commercially bred in the Far East by fish farmers and as such is widely available among Singapore shipments in its albino form. Malayan 'wild' forms are described as green to dark brown with reddish margins.

In its natural habitat (where some albinoism occurs) eggs are deposited in holes about 250mm (10in) long made in the pond bank below the water surface. It is estimated that between 2000 and 15,000 fry are raised in each nest.

In Florida and several other States of America, the Walking Catfish is banned because of its introduction into native waters. Wild stories of giant specimens attacking pet dogs and confusing car drivers at night by walking across roads are exaggerated. However, the introduction of stock by storm flooding into the Everglades is said to pose a threat to native fishes.

Clarotes laticeps

False Chrysichthys
- **Habitat:** Tributaries of the Blue and White Nile, Niger and Chad basins
- **Length:** 600mm (24in)
- **Diet:** Crustaceans and fish

Above: **Clarotes laticeps**
Although a deadly predator, this catfish will live happily among large community fishes and will adapt quickly to taking aquarium foods.

- **Sex differences:** Males possess a slightly longer adipose fin and have a more slender body than females
- **Aquarium compatibility:** Suitable only among large robust fishes
- **Aquarium breeding:** Not known

A rare catfish among River Niger imports, *Clarotes* is identified by its distinctive adipose fin, sometimes

Below: **Euchilichthys guentheri**
A close relative of Chiloglanis *sp., this catfish enjoys the same bright, well-aerated water conditions.*

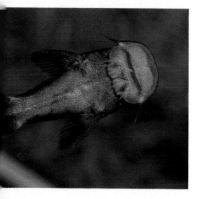

known as a second dorsal. The white-tipped tail fin makes this catfish attractive, although its predatory nature restricts *Clarotes* from most community systems.

Euchilichthys guentheri
False Chiloglanis; False Suckermouth
- **Habitat:** Fast-flowing streams on the Zaire River
- **Length:** 100mm (4in)
- **Diet:** Insect larvae, algae and small crustaceans
- **Sex differences:** Not known
- **Aquarium compatibility:** Non-aggressive, although territorial towards its own kind. An interesting species suitable for most communities
- **Aquarium breeding:** Not known

The first *Euchilichthys* imported from Zaire were mistaken for giant *Chiloglanis*, to which they bear a remarkable resemblance. The False Suckermouth has a longer head, nostrils set close together and a free border to the eye.
The difficulty in keeping both types of African Suckermouth Catfishes relates totally to their natural habitat requirements. In the aquarium they tend to suffer from too low a pH (it should be around 7.0), oxygen deficiency and an incorrect diet. Frozen larvae, bloodworm and *Daphnia* will provide a suitably balanced diet.

Above: **Eutropiellus vanderweyeri**
Distinguished from closely related species by the caudal-lobe stripes.

Eutropiellus vanderweyeri

African Glass Catfish
- **Habitat:** Fast-flowing rivers of the River Niger system
- **Length:** 75mm (3in)
- **Diet:** Insect larvae – but will adapt well to prepared flake foods and other aquarium diets
- **Sex differences:** Females are deeper in the body than males
- **Aquarium compatibility:** Relatively peaceful to all fishes.
- **Aquarium breeding:** Not known

This species is often referred to as *E. debauwi*, although this identification is said to be very doubtful. A second species is imported from Zaire which appears similar to the African Glass Catfish but may well be the true *debauwi*.

These catfishes are excellent midwater shoalers for medium-sized to large community aquariums.

Hemisynodontis membranaceus

Moustache Catfish
- **Habitat:** The major African rivers
- **Length:** 300mm (12in)
- **Diet:** Plant and animal plankton in the wild; suitable prepared foods in the aquarium
- **Sex differences:** Not known
- **Aquarium compatibility:** Relatively peaceful towards all fishes
- **Aquarium breeding:** Not known

Hemisynodontis had been merely a name in scientific literature until the shipment of this and many other interesting catfishes from the Niger in 1983. The broad maxillary barbels, from which the author has derived the common name 'Moustache Catfish', are used as a scoop to direct animal plankton and plant plankton into the fish's mouth. Very fine gill, or branchial, spines act as filters to extract even the finest food from the water flow.

Only a few specimens have been kept in captivity and these have adapted well to prepared foods.

Heteroptneustes fossilis

Stinging or Liver Catfish
- **Habitat:** Widespread across Asia in pools, ditches, rivers and lakes
- **Length:** 300mm (12in)
- **Diet:** Any insect or crustacean foods. Juveniles and adult specimens feed well on pellets, foodsticks and prawns or earthworms

Above:
Hemisynodontis membranaceus
A Synodontis with large maxillary barbels. Provide a large aquarium.

- **Sex differences:** Males are more slender and often more attractively patterned than females, sometimes with yellow lateral stripes
- **Aquarium compatibility:** Suitable for a community of large fishes, but predatory towards small fishes
- **Aquarium breeding:** Aquarium spawnings are known but unrecorded; habitat accounts are available, however

Available under several common names, including the Liver, Fossil and Stinging Catfish, captive specimens of this species adapt well to life in the aquarium. Large specimens have prominent dorsal and pectoral fin-spines, which are said to be spiked with a mild venom.

These fishes spawn in the rainy season, placing yellowish eggs in depressions, or nests, hollowed out by the pair. Adults show parental care beyond the hatching and free-swimming stage of the fry.

Below: **Heteroptneustes fossilis**
Possibly confused with the Walking Catfish but more slender in shape.

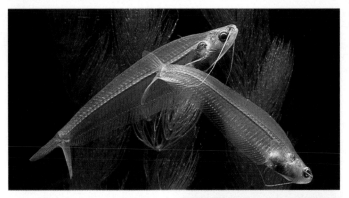

Above: **Kryptopterus bicirrhis**
Although delicate in appearance, this midwater shoaling catfish can be kept with community fishes.

Kryptopterus bicirrhis
Glass Catfish
- **Habitat:** Widespread in Asian rivers
- **Length:** 100mm (4in)
- **Diet:** General aquatic larvae, but will accept dried foods in the aquarium
- **Sex differences:** Not known
- **Aquarium compatibility:** Suitable for any small-fish community system
- **Aquarium breeding:** Not known

This shoaling, midwater catfish is found in great numbers in the wild. It rarely reaches the adult size in the aquarium, however, and often falls foul of aggression from other tank inhabitants. Unlike most catfishes, this species is diurnal, i.e. active during the daylight hours.

The Glass Catfish is commercially farmed in the Far East, but the exact details of spawning are unrecorded.

Leiocassis siamensis
Bumblebee Catfish
- **Habitat:** Rivers and creeks of Thailand
- **Length:** 150mm (6in)
- **Diet:** Shrimp, insect larvae, snails. Will thrive on frozen shrimp and bloodworms, and will adapt to prepared foods
- **Sex differences:** Males are slender by comparison with the

deeper bodied females
- **Aquarium compatibility:** Young specimens are relatively safe to keep among general community species, although adult fishes should not be kept with small tetras or livebearing fishes.
- **Aquarium breeding:** Not known

The Asian Bumblebee Catfish is well known among catfish enthusiasts and is often the first 'unusual' species encountered by fishkeepers. Large specimens are clearly night prowlers, capable of consuming resting diurnal fishes. Take great care, therefore, not to introduce this species into a community of small fishes.

Leiocassis stenomus
False Bumblebee Catfish
- **Habitat:** Rivers and creeks of southeastern Thailand and Indonesia
- **Length:** 100-125mm (4-5in)
- **Diet:** Crustaceans and insect

Below: **Leiocassis stenomus**
Smaller and less brightly patterned than the true Bumblebee Catfish.

Bottom: **Leiocassis siamensis**
This sleek and attractive catfish is a favourite species with fishkeepers.

larvae. Will thrive on frozen shrimp and bloodworm, and will adapt to taking prepared foods
- **Sex differences:** As in *Leiocassis siamensis*
- **Aquarium compatibility:** As in *Leiocassis siamensis*
- **Aquarium breeding:** Not known

The False Bumblebee is not often encountered in comparison with *L.siamensis*, and usually only finds its way into aquarium shops via saltwater/freshwater shipments from Indonesia.

Above: **Lophiobagrus cyclurus**
An ideal 'scavenger' for an African Rift Valley community aquarium.

Lophiobagrus cyclurus
Tanganyikan Dwarf Bagrid
- **Habitat:** The shoreline rubble of Lake Tanganyika
- **Length:** 100mm (4in)
- **Diet:** Small shrimp, chopped earthworms, bloodworm and flake food
- **Sex differences:** Females are larger and generally more robust than males
- **Aquarium compatibility:** Excellent for a Tanganyikan cichlid community – keeps very much to itself
- **Aquarium breeding:** A pair dig out a hollow in the sand or gravel underneath rocks or cavework. They spawn in the cave, producing 30-40 eggs which are then cared for until they hatch. Fry can be raised easily on brineshrimp and powdered flake.

Lophiobagrus are said to produce a poisonous body slime that can kill other fishes if kept in a confined space with them. This unproved factor should not detract from the ideal aquarium compatibility and breeding opportunity this species offers. There are no records of problems with this catfish in the aquarium and the author has kept them together with Tanganyikan cichlids without any difficulty.

Below: **Malapterurus electricus**
Young specimens such as this are very adaptable in aquariums; adults feed on any fish they can cope with. The Electric Catfish has 'batteries' in the form of a jacket wrapped around the trunk. A fascinating fish.

Malapterurus electricus
Electric Catfish
- **Habitat:** Widespread in rivers and pools of tropical Africa
- **Length:** 850mm (34in)
- **Diet:** Fish. Aquarium specimens will adapt to feeding on large earthworms, prawns and various land creatures, such as beetles.
- **Sex differences:** Males are slender in comparison to females
- **Aquarium compatibility:** Keep only with the most robust *Tilapia* type of cichlids
- **Aquarium breeding:** Not known

The electric organs are in the sides of the fish and extend for most of the body length. The head is negative and the tail positive, and the

Above: **Mochokiella paynei**
This forest stream catfish, with distinctive feathered barbels, is ideally suited to small aquariums.

electrical discharges, stored in the body muscles (adapted as electroplates), are used for defence and for stunning prey. The Electric Catfish can emit a range of shocks, from short pulses to massive 250-volt discharges.

Most imported specimens are destined for public aquariums or zoo exhibitions, although as exotic and curious animals they are kept by a few fishkeepers with a desire to celebrate the unusual.

Mochokiella paynei
Payne's Catfish
- **Habitat:** Slow acidic creeks in West Africa
- **Length:** 75mm (3in)
- **Diet:** Larval and crustacean foods in the wild. Will accept a wide range of aquarium foods
- **Sex differences:** Females are rounder than males
- **Aquarium compatibility:** An excellent community catfish
- **Aquarium breeding:** Not known

First discovered in 1979 in a forest creek in Sierra Leone by Dr. Payne, this dwarf catfish has proved extremely popular with fishkeepers. The branched barbels are a good identification feature, although they are superficially similar to those of the closely related *Synodontis* sp.

Mystus armatus

One-spot Catfish; Pearl Catfish
- **Habitat:** India, Burma, possibly Thailand
- **Length:** 125mm (5in)
- **Diet:** Crustaceans, insect larvae, etc. Will accept suitable aquarium foods
- **Sex differences:** Males are smaller and more slender in the body than females
- **Aquarium compatibility:** Juvenile *Mystus* are fairly peaceful towards community fishes. It is only when they attain more adult proportions that they begin to predate on small fishes. Predation usually occurs at night, when these catfishes are active
- **Aquarium breeding:** The Pearl Catfish was the first *Mystus* species to be spawned in the aquarium. Several females and a single male were introduced into a cool freshwater aquarium containing plants but no substrate. Early the following morning, the females produced several hundred eggs, of which at least one hundred proved fertile. Fry development was quite rapid; within days the youngsters could be seen swimming freely

Despite their predatory tendencies when adult, this species is well suited to larger Asian communities containing large barbs, gouramis and other catfishes, or South American communities containing cichlids, large characins and catfishes. As shoaling fishes they are best kept in small groups of four to six individuals. In a group they will feed across the substrate, taking a broad range of prepared, freeze-dried and frozen foods.

Mystus micracanthus

Two-spot Catfish
- **Habitat:** Sumatra, Java, Borneo and Thailand
- **Length:** 125mm (5in)
- **Diet:** Crustacean foods, shrimps, etc. Will accept aquarium foods
- **Sex differences:** Males are smaller and more slender in the body than females
- **Aquarium compatibility:** Not safe with very small fishes, although they are ideally suited to an Asian-style community aquarium containing barbs and gouramis
- **Aquarium breeding:** As in *Mystus armatus*

The Two-spot Catfish was available in aquarium circles without a scientific name until a connection was made to a description of

Below: **Mystus armatus**
These juveniles, illustrated with an adult, are from the first successful aquarium spawning of this species.

Above: **Mystus micracanthus**
Catfish enthusiasts agree that the Two-spot Catfish is one of the most attractive Mystus *species.*

Mystus micracanthus by the ichthyologist Bleeker, in 1846. The artist's impression at that time showed a catfish without any obvious markings, although another researcher in the early 1940s described it with two body spots.

It is one of the most attractively coloured species within the genus and will thrive in a neutral system.

Mystus nemurus
Asian Red-tailed Catfish
- **Habitat:** Found in rivers throughout Asia, even into tidal systems
- **Length:** 600mm (24in)
- **Diet:** Crustaceans, fish, insects, etc. Suitable aquarium foods
- **Sex differences:** Not known

- **Aquarium compatibility:** An aggressive species capable of stripping the fins off other fishes, especially other catfishes. Suitable for very spacious aquariums with large cichlids and barbs, etc.
- **Aquarium breeding:** Not known

The Asian Red-tailed Catfish has been available among Thailand shipments over recent years and has sometimes been offered in place of the much sought after South American Red-tailed Catfish, *Phractocephalus.*

Several colour varieties are recorded, the caudal fin being red, orange or even yellow.

Below: **Mystus nemurus**
The tail coloration is known to vary a great deal, although this, the red-tailed form, is the one most widely available in the aquarium hobby.

Above: **Mystus vittatus**
Deep-bodied specimens, as shown here, are likely to be females. The males are slender by comparison.

Mystus vittatus
Pyjama Catfish
- **Habitat:** Creeks and rivers throughout tropical Asia
- **Length:** 125-150mm (5-6in)
- **Diet:** Small aquatic insects, fish fry and larval foods in the wild. Will accept a wide range of aquarium foods
- **Sex differences:** Males are smaller and more slender than females
- **Aquarium compatibility:** Predatory towards smaller fishes, but suitable for larger cichlid/barb communities
- **Aquarium breeding:** Egg scatterers

This is one of the best-known Asian catfishes, although many aquarium books seem to overlook the fact. It was spawned in the aquarium for the first time in 1985 by an East German aquarist, Dr. Hans Franke. Of the several thousand eggs produced, a high percentage hatched after several days.

Mystus wykii
Crystal-eyed Catfish
- **Habitat:** Thailand, Sumatra and Java
- **Length:** 600-750mm (24-30in)
- **Diet:** Live fish, prawns, earthworms
- **Sex differences:** Not known
- **Aquarium compatibility:** A lone predator, unsuited to any community system, although a public aquarium could provide sufficient territory
- **Aquarium breeding:** Not known

The Crystal-eyed Catfish is said to have mystical qualities according to Thai fishermen, who call it Plakotkao. In aquariums, it proves to be one of the most aggressive species of all catfishes, and is certainly unafraid of man. According to research, it is extremely rare in Thailand waters, where aquarium specimens are collected from the largest tidal rivers.

Pangasius sutchi
Asian Shark Catfish
- **Habitat:** Large rivers in Thailand
- **Length:** 450mm (18in)
- **Diet:** In the wild, this species consumes fruit and vegetation,

Below: **Mystus wykii**
A 60cm (24in) specimen, able to attack and kill fish up to half its size.

Above: **Pangasius sutchii**
Adapted to live in fast-flowing rivers, the Shark Catfish should be kept in a reasonably large aquarium.

insect larvae, shrimp and various other crustaceans. In the aquarium, it takes bloodworm, foodsticks, frozen krill and Gamma shrimp, chopped earthworms, and spinach
● **Sex differences:** Males have darker stripes and are more slender than females
● **Aquarium compatibility:** Ideal for a large-fish community system, but should be kept in small groups
● **Aquarium breeding:** Not known

Asian Shark Catfishes – now also available in a 'blonde' form – are usually kept as individual fishes in aquariums, which does not encourage them to settle in captivity. They shoal in large numbers in the major Asian rivers, especially in stretches of rapids. They can be extremely nervous in aquariums, and will cause a great deal of damage to themselves by striking the cover glass and tank sides, etc., if disturbed. Although they are generally available as youngsters farm bred in the Far East, even small specimens only 50-75mm (2-3in) long are not suitable for inclusion in small systems. This is a catfish for large aquariums.

Parauchenoglanis macrostoma
Dwarf Giraffe Catfish
● **Habitat:** West African creeks
● **Length:** 200mm (8in)
● **Diet:** Larval and crustacean foods in the wild. Will accept a wide range of aquarium foods
● **Sex differences:** Not known
● **Aquarium compatibility:** Not suitable for a community aquarium with very small fishes. An ideal scavenger for a cichlid community containing fishes 75-100mm (3.5-4in) long
● **Aquarium breeding:** Not known

This dwarf catfish is seasonally available from Africa, but is not well known among fishkeepers. Keep it in large groups; individuals can be aggressively territorial.

Below:
Parauchenoglanis macrostoma
A juvenile of this scarce species.

Synodontis afrofischeri
Fischer's Catfish
- **Habitat:** Lake Victoria, Nile basin
- **Length:** 125-150mm (5-6in)
- **Diet:** Crustaceans, insect larvae, plant debris and terrestrial insects. Aquarium specimens will accept frozen Gamma shrimp, brineshrimp and *Mysis* shrimp, leaf spinach, chopped earthworms, foodsticks and pellets, frozen or freeze-dried bloodworm, gnat larvae and mosquito larvae.
- **Sex differences:** Not known
- **Aquarium compatibility:** This species will adapt to a wide range of water chemistry (acidic-alkaline systems) and mixes with most aquarium fishes
- **Aquarium breeding:** Not known

A study of this species in Lake Victoria proved the species to be sexually mature at 75mm (3in) and a high percentage of the females to be

Above: **Synodontis afrofischeri**
This river and lake species accepts a wide range of water conditions.

constantly carrying eggs. Spawning occurs in peaks between January and August/September in pre- or post-rainy season surges. It is suggested that the spawning peaks are part of a reproductive strategy that serves to synchronize reproductive activity with increased food and favourable spawning and rearing areas prior to or following the rains, which occur in March-June and October-November.

Adult females produce between 200 and 15,000 eggs. Should an aquarium spawning occur, the lucky fishkeeper would have an incredible number of fry to raise!

Below: **Synodontis alberti**
A young specimen that is distinctly patterned and clearly large-eyed. Both are good recognition points.

Synodontis alberti
Albert's Catfish
- **Habitat:** Zaire River
- **Length:** 150mm (6in)
- **Diet:** Crustaceans, insect larvae, etc. Aquarium specimens will accept flake food, frozen bloodworm, *Daphnia*, gnat and mosquito larvae, brine shrimp; finely chopped earthworms, pellets and foodsticks
- **Sex differences:** Adult male specimens retain a slight giraffe-like body pattern, whereas larger and more robust females lose this pattern as the body finally fades to a light grey
- **Aquarium compatibility:** An excellent community catfish suitable for almost any tropical system
- **Aquarium breeding:** Not known

The large eye and long sweeping maxillary barbel enable this species to be easily recognized. As one of the smaller *Synodontis*, Albert's Catfish can be accommodated in any modest aquarium. Juveniles display a particularly attractive silver body, ornately patterned with large spots, as shown opposite.

Synodontis angelicus
Polka-dot Catfish
- **Habitat:** Rivers on the main Zaire system
- **Length:** 200mm (8in)

Above: **Synodontis angelicus**
One of the best-known Synodontis species available to fishkeepers and much sought after by enthusiasts.

- **Diet:** In the wild, this species takes insect larvae, fish fry, terrestrial insects, plant debris and shrimp. In the aquarium, it will accept flake foods, frozen bloodworm, *Mysis* shrimp and brineshrimp, chopped earthworms, and pellets or foodsticks
- **Sex differences:** Females are larger and more robust in the body, and develop a drab body colour in maturity as the white patterning fades. Males are slightly smaller, slender in the body and retain some of the white spots as adults.
- **Aquarium compatibility:** Semi-adult specimens are territorial. Safe with small community fishes
- **Aquarium breeding:** Unknown

The Polka-dot Catfish was once the most sought after species among fishkeepers. The black body, spotted in yellow or white dots, offers an attractive pattern – often lacking in catfishes. Different populations have distinct patterns. One form with a combination of stripes, bars and spots was originally thought to be a subspecies, *S.angelicus zonatus*.

Synodontis aterrimus
False Nigriventris; Dark Synodontis
- **Habitat:** Zaire rivers
- **Length:** 100mm (4in)
- **Diet:** In the wild, this species lives on insect larvae and terrestrial insects that have fallen into the water. In the aquarium it will accept bloodworm, *Daphnia*, mosquito and gnat larvae (freeze-dried or frozen), and floating foodsticks
- **Sex differences:** Females are larger than males
- **Aquarium compatibility:** An ideal community catfish suitable for small community systems
- **Aquarium breeding:** Not known

This dwarf species is marginally similar to *Synodontis nigriventris*, well known to fishkeepers as the Upside-down Catfish. The latter is slightly smaller and lighter in colour than *Synodontis aterrimus*, however. Both species are true inverting catfish and possess dark ventral surfaces that provide effective camouflage. *Synodontis* species that spend a high percentage of their time swimming upside-down are usually surface feeders on hatching fly larvae.

Synodontis brichardi
Brichard's Catfish
- **Habitat:** Zaire River
- **Length:** 125-150mm (5-6in)
- **Diet:** In the habitat, this fish lives on shrimp, and possibly algae and insect larvae. Aquarium

Above: **Synodontis aterrimus**
A true inverting species ideal for small aquariums. Provide a suitable diet for its surface-feeding habits.

specimens will feed on Gamma shrimp, brineshrimp and *Mysis* shrimp, chopped leaf spinach and foodsticks.
- **Sex differences:** Not known
- **Aquarium compatibility:** Extremely peaceful towards other species. Can sometimes be the target for aggressive species
- **Aquarium breeding:** Not known

A mainstay of Zaire fish exports along with *Synodontis decorus*, the Banded or Brichard's Catfish is extremely popular among enthusiasts. Its streamlined body, unusual in this group, suggests that it is a fast-water fish and will therefore flourish in a bright, fresh system of pH 6.9-7.5 with plenty of aeration. Aquarium specimens will accept shredded leaf spinach, which may indicate a need to provide a 'green base' to their diet.

Synodontis camelopardalis
Giraffe Synodontis
- **Habitat:** Zaire River and pools
- **Length:** 150mm (6in)
- **Diet:** Its feeding habits in the wild are not known, but it probably lives on a typical catfish 'opportunist' diet. In the aquarium, offer it shrimp,

Above: **Synodontis brichardi**
The streamlined shape is a clear adaptation to life in the fast-flowing waters of the Zaire River.

bloodworm, flake, pellets and/or foodsticks
● **Sex differences:** Not known
● **Aquarium compatibility:** Reasonably peaceful towards most fishes and ideally suited to medium-sized communities
● **Aquarium breeding:** Not known

This is one of the rarer species, found among the Zaire imports and relatively unknown among fishkeepers. The blotched, giraffe-like pattern is similar to that of

Synodontis alberti, although *Synodontis camelopardalis* is a much more slender catfish.

As in most *Synodontis* species, the strong juvenile pattern fades as the fishes mature, but this is one of the most attractive of the lesser known species.

Synodontis camelopardalis is also confused with *Synodontis caudalis*, but the latter grows larger, is more robust and displays caudal filament extensions.

Below:
Synodontis camelopardalis
An adult specimen of this relatively unfamiliar species. The juvenile pattern has faded with maturity.

Synodontis caudalis

Whiptail Synodontis; Whiptail Catfish

- **Habitat:** Zaire River and pools
- **Length:** 200mm (8in)
- **Diet:** Little is known about its natural diet, but it is likely to be typically wide ranging. Aquarium specimens accept shrimp, bloodworm, flake, pellet and foodsticks
- **Sex differences:** Not known
- **Aquarium compatibility:** Fairly peaceful towards other community fishes. Can sometimes be territorial towards other *Synodontis* species
- **Aquarium breeding:** Not known

The Whiptail Catfish is so named by the author because of its characteristic extensions to the tail fin. Its body pattern and shape resemble those of *Synodontis camelopardalis* from the same region, although the Whiptail grows larger and has a much darker, almost reticulated pattern.

Synodontis clarias

Red-tailed Synodontis

- **Habitat:** West and Central African rivers
- **Length:** 200mm (8in)
- **Diet:** Crustaceans, algae and

Above: **Synodontis caudalis**
Mistaken for Synodontis robertsi *for many years until the latter fish was made available in Zaire fish imports.*

insect larvae. Will accept a wide range of aquarium foods
- **Sex differences:** Males possess a more acutely pointed humeral process – a gill spine situated at either side of the head

Below: **Synodontis clarias**
The red caudal fin characterizes this species from all others in the genus. It is possible to keep this boisterous catfish with similarly sized fishes.

fishkeepers, however, until exports from the Niger system in recent years. The distinctively branched barbels probably help this species to locate food in its natural habitat.

Synodontis decorus
Clown Catfish
- **Habitat:** Zaire rivers and pools
- **Length:** 300mm (12in)
- **Diet:** Crustaceans, algae and insect larvae in the wild, but will accept aquarium foods
- **Sex differences:** Males are more slender than females and have a darker pattern
- **Aquarium compatibility:** Juveniles are peaceful, although semi-adult specimens can be extremely disruptive to smaller community systems
- **Aquarium breeding:** Not known

- **Aquarium compatibility:** A robust species showing territorial aggression but compatible with similarly sized fishes
- **Aquarium breeding:** Not known

The Red-tailed Synodontis has the distinction of being the first of over one hundred species to be described to science – in 1758 – and therefore is the type for the genus. It was relatively rare among

The Clown Catfish is one of the most popular species of all the African catfishes because of its attractive body and fin patterning, and also because it is often available. Large specimens are known to develop a whiplike extension of the dorsal fin, which sometimes reaches as far back as the caudal fin.

Adults tend to be less active than juveniles and often become very secretive during daylight hours.

Below: **Synodontis decorus**
A juvenile of this popular African catfish. Dorsal fin extensions develop in adults of both sexes.

Synodontis dhonti
False Spotted Catfish
- **Habitat:** Lake Tanganyika
- **Length:** 400mm (16in)
- **Diet:** Crustacean and insect larvae in the wild, but will take aquarium foods
- **Sex differences:** Females larger and more robust in the body than males
- **Aquarium compatibility:** Territorial towards other *Synodontis* sp., but relatively peaceful with Rift Valley Lake cichlids
- **Aquarium breeding:** Not known; alkaline system required

The aquarium compatibility information is based on the presumption that this species behaves in the same way as the other species of *Synodontis* found in Lake Tanganyika.

Above: **Synodontis dhonti**
Imports from Lake Tanganyika offer this rarity. Juveniles, as here, can be confused with S. multipunctatus.

Below: **Synodontis eupterus**
This adult displays the 'feathered' dorsal fin that gives this species its name of Feather Fin Catfish.

Above: **Synodontis eurystomus**
*A striking species justly popular
among enthusiasts. A snail-feeder
from the shores of Lake Tanganyika.*

Strangely, several other Lake
Tanganyikan species share an
almost identical colour pattern to
the juvenile *Synodontis dhonti*, but
the False Spotted Catfish loses its
colour pattern in adulthood and
becomes plain grey. In its juvenile
colour it resembles *Synodontis
multipunctatus*, a commonly
imported species from Lake
Tanganyika which reaches half its
size. (See page 66 for details.)

Synodontis eupterus
Feather Fin Catfish
- **Habitat:** Niger River system
- **Length:** 150-200mm (6-8in)
- **Diet:** In the aquarium, this
  species will accept frozen shrimp
  and bloodworm, flake, tablet and
  foodsticks
- **Sex differences:** Females are
  generally more robust than males
- **Aquarium compatibility:** A
  peaceful species ideally suited to
  most medium-sized to large
  community systems
- **Aquarium breeding:** Not known

The Feather Fin Catfish is very
similar to *Synodontis nigrita*, but
less common. The latter species
lacks the distinctive dorsal fin
extensions, although juvenile

Synodontis eupterus do not display
them either. Young specimens can
be distinguished by the presence of
a high, long-based adipose fin.

This attractively patterned
species is ideal for a large cichlid
community, where it will feed on the
left-overs created by messy feeders
in the waters above them.

Synodontis eurystomus
(S. polli)
Leopard Catfish
- **Habitat:** The rocky shoreline of
  Lake Tanganyika
- **Length:** 150mm (6in)
- **Diet:** Crustaceans, snails and
  algae in the wild; will accept most
  aquarium foods
- **Sex differences:** Females reach
  the full stated length of 150mm
  (6in); males usually reach only
  125mm (5in)
- **Aquarium compatibility:**
  Peaceful except with its own kind
  or species that most resemble it
- **Aquarium breeding:** Not known;
  an alkaline system required

The dark leopard markings of this
species commend it to catfish
enthusiasts. It is collected with the
Pygmy Leopard Catfish, *Synodontis
petricolor*, which is adult at 100mm
(4in) and often confused with it. Both
species are specialized snail
feeders, although in aquariums they
will accept a wide range of frozen
and prepared foods.

Synodontis filamentosus
Filament Catfish
- **Habitat:** Nile, Niger and Volta River systems
- **Length:** 200-230mm (8-9in)
- **Diet:** Its natural diet is not known, but is probably typically wide ranging. In the aquarium, both small and large specimens will accept a wide range of prepared foods, including flake, foodsticks and pellets, and also crustacean foods (frozen or freeze-dried). Larval foods and chopped earthworms are also accepted, along with the occasional green food, such as chopped leaf spinach and lettuce
- **Sex differences:** Not known

Above: **Synodontis filamentosus**
This mature specimen displays the dorsal filament that justifies its scientific name. It is known to have a highly variable body colour pattern.

- **Aquarium compatibility:** An aggressive species suitable for keeping only in large-fish community systems. It is boisterous to other *Synodontis*, especially its own kind
- **Aquarium breeding:** Not known

Below: **Synodontis flavitaeniatus**
The golden-yellow body stripes are an outstanding feature of young specimens. They have ensured its popularity among enthusiasts.

A long-bodied, robust species encountered among River Niger collections. The caudal lobe stripes and dorsal extension aid identification, although the body patterning can be highly variable.

Synodontis flavitaeniatus

Pyjamas Catfish

- **Habitat:** Zaire Rivers and pools
- **Length:** 200mm (8in)
- **Diet:** The natural diet has not been recorded, but is probably typical of *Synodontis*. Juvenile and adult aquarium specimens will accept a wide range of foods, including frozen insect and crustacean foods, flake, pellet and foodsticks, tablet foods and shrimps
- **Sex differences:** Adult females are deeper in the body than males and usually display a plain body
- **Aquarium compatibility:** Peaceful towards most fishes although it can be territorial to its own kind
- **Aquarium breeding:** Not known

Below: **Synodontis greshoffi**
Although superficially similar to several other Synodontis *species, the large eye, prominent adipose fin and long barbels are characteristic.*

The Pyjamas Catfish has a unique and striking colour pattern of horizontal yellow and brown stripes. It is a much sought after species that still commands a high price.

A public aquarium in Holland boasts a twenty year-old specimen, a pointer to the longevity of many catfishes in captivity.

Synodontis greshoffi

Greshoff's Catfish

- **Habitat:** Zaire Rivers and pools
- **Length:** 200mm (8in)
- **Diet:** This species is a typical opportunist feeder and will accept prepared foods, flake, pellet, foodsticks and tablets. Enhance this 'dried' diet with alternate offerings of frozen insect larvae and crustacean foods
- **Sex differences:** Not known
- **Aquarium compatibility:** An ideal community species
- **Aquarium breeding:** Not known

Greshoff's Catfish is often confused with other *Synodontis* species, although its large eye, deep body and large adipose fin are distinctive characteristics. The long maxillary barbels clearly identify the species, however. When not pointing ahead, these stretch back along the body to reach the ventral fins.

Above: **Synodontis koensis**
A relatively small species with a variable colour pattern and indistinct adipose fin.

Synodontis koensis

Ko River Catfish
- **Habitat:** Rivers, Ivory Coast
- **Length:** 100-150mm (4-6in)
- **Diet:** Insect larvae, terrestrial insects, crustaceans and general plant and organic debris. Suitable aquarium foods can be substituted for this natural diet
- **Sex differences:** Males have a more acutely pointed humeral spine, a darker colour pattern and a larger adipose fin than females
- **Aquarium compatibility:** A small, peaceful species
- **Aquarium breeding:** Not known

This small to medium-sized species is sometimes encountered through West African imports into Europe. The colour pattern is extremely variable, even among population groups and between males and females. It is remarkably similar in appearance to another West African species, *Synodontis tourei*, which the author tentatively suggests is a form of *Synodontis koensis*.

Synodontis multipunctatus

Many-spotted Catfish
- **Habitat:** The rocky and sandy shoreline of Lake Tanganyika
- **Length:** Males 200mm (8in); females 280mm (11in)
- **Diet:** Crustaceans, algae and insect larvae. Will accept suitable aquarium foods

- **Sex differences:** Males may possess longer pectoral spines and tend to be smaller than females
- **Aquarium compatibility:** Perfect for African Rift Valley Lake cichlid community systems. Generally peaceful, but can be territorial towards its own species
- **Aquarium breeding:** A 'cuckoo' relationship is known to exist between this catfish and mouthbrooding cichlids, which has led to some fry being raised in aquariums.

A popular export from the Burundi district of Lake Tanganyika, *Synodontis multipunctatus* is undoubtedly one of the world's most attractive catfishes. It is often confused with *Synodontis petricolor*, which is smaller; *Synodontis eurystomus*, which is also smaller but also has a darker body pattern; and *Synodontis dhonti*, which grows larger and loses the beautiful spots and body stripes as it becomes mature.

Its main diet in Lake Tanganyika is certainly snails (applicable to most of the Rift Valley Lake species mentioned) and this crustacean part of the diet can be made up by frozen foods, such as Gamma shrimp, brineshrimp and *Mysis*.

Synodontis multipunctatus will thrive in an alkaline system (pH 7.5-8.2) with a good rock aquascape alongside Lake Tanganyikan and Lake Malawi cichlids. Two individuals will clash over territorial claims, and so it is wise to keep them singly or in groups of three or

Above:
Synodontis multipunctatus
*No two specimens share the same
pattern, which makes this one of the
most intriguing* Synodontis *species.*

more to prevent bullying.

During cichlid spawnings, these
catfishes are known to swim
between the pair, eating expelled
cichlid eggs and replacing some
with their own. The mouthbrooding
female cichlid is then said to pick up
the catfish eggs alongside her own.
Although the catfish eggs are less
than half the size of the cichlid eggs,
which are 3-4mm (0.12-0.16in)
across, the female is said to mistake
the catfish eggs for her own.
Aquarists have suggested the
catfish fry hatch in the cichlid's
mouth. The catfishes develop
faster, hatch and then predate on
the later cichlid hatchlings. This
assumption arises from the lower fry
numbers produced by females
known to be raising catfish fry
together with their own.

Synodontis nigrita
*Dark-spotted Catfish; False Upside-
down Catfish*
- **Habitat:** Widespread in the rivers
  of West and Central Africa
- **Length:** 200mm (8in)
- **Diet:** Almost all foods accepted
- **Sex differences:** Males are
  slender in comparison with
  females
- **Aquarium compatibility:**
  Somewhat boisterous as it grows
  to the semi-adult size; more
  suited to a medium-sized to large
  cichlid community
- **Aquarium breeding:** Not known

At 50mm (2in), *Synodontis nigrita* is
often sold as the 'Upside-down
Catfish', and many fishkeepers
would believe they are purchasing
the true Upside-down Catfish,

Below: **Synodontis nigrita**
*One of the most commonly
imported species from Nigeria. It is
distinguishable from other closely
related forms by its many spots.*

Synodontis nigriventris. The latter species is a true inverting dwarf catfish, however, and adult at half the size of Synodontis nigrita.

This is an inexpensive African catfish suitable for a wide range of water conditions and fish communities, except for small community systems containing livebearing fishes or small tetras. The juvenile to semi-adult growth rate is extremely fast, and they are then likely to attack slow-moving fishes with ornate finnage, especially at night.

Synodontis nigriventris
Upside-down Catfish
- **Habitat:** Zaire and Niger River systems
- **Length:** 100mm (4in)
- **Diet:** Larval foods in the wild, but will take most aquarium foods
- **Sex differences:** Females are deeper bodied than males
- **Aquarium compatibility:** An ideal small aquarium catfish, suitable for almost every community system
- **Aquarium breeding:** Aquarium successes are known but accounts are vague. Parent fishes are said to spawn into a depression in the gravel and show some parental care

The Upside-down Catfish is one of *the* most popular aquarium catfishes and has been imported in huge numbers into the USA and

Above: **Synodontis nigriventris**
A well-known catfish in the hobby, shown here in its usual inverted position. Widely compatible.

Europe for many years. They are ideal shoaling fishes, well suited to life in aquariums, and will accept a wide range of prepared foods. A group of fishes will appreciate some floating bark or surface plants under which to conceal themselves.

As inverting species, they feed on insect life at the water surface and are darker on the ventral surface for camouflage. (This is opposite to the shading in normally orientated fishes, in which the upper, or dorsal, surface is usually darker than the lower, or ventral surface.)

Below: **Synodontis njassae**
This is the only Synodontis species from Lake Malawi. Two colour forms – large-spot and small-spot – exist.

Synodontis njassae
Malawi Catfish
- **Habitat:** The rocky shoreline of Lake Malawi
- **Length:** 150mm (6in)
- **Diet:** Crustaceans in the wild; will accept aquarium foods
- **Sex differences:** Females are more robust than males
- **Aquarium compatibility:** Ideal for any Rift Valley Lake cichlid community system
- **Aquarium breeding:** Not known

Synodontis njassae, the only *Synodontis* species available from Lake Malawi, is an extremely adaptable catfish, being able to survive extreme conditions – pH range 6.6-8.5, for example. It is vaguely confused in literature with *Synodontis multipunctatus* from Lake Tanganyika, but it lacks the white edges to the fins that are characteristic of the latter species.

The Malawi *Synodontis* was once plentiful in imports, although in recent times it appears somewhat scarce. The body colour pattern and spots vary, especially from juvenile to adult stage; young specimens display many small spots on a pale brown body, whereas adults generally show a dark brown body with a few large spots.

Synodontis notatus
One-spot Catfish
- **Habitat:** Zaire River
- **Length:** 250mm (10in)
- **Diet:** Aquarium specimens will consume a wide variety of prepared foods. They will thrive if offered standard frozen insect and crustacean foods, chopped leaf spinach, and dried foods
- **Sex differences:** Males are slender, possess longer pectoral spines and longer caudal fin lobes than females.
- **Aquarium compatibility:** Juveniles are reasonably peaceful towards community fishes, but semi-adults can be disruptive and boisterous
- **Aquarium breeding:** Not known

The large spot pattern of this species is quite variable; in one survey of 100 specimens, 15 percent displayed extra body spots, usually two and three spots. *Synodontis notatus* was once available in large numbers, but recent Zaire shipments have shown it to be less plentiful.

Below: **Synodontis notatus**
The spots on the body can vary in number, but this specimen displays the usual one spot on either side.

Above: **Synodontis ocellifer**
The large-spot form shown here is the most attractive of several colour forms known to exist in this species.

Synodontis ocellifer
Large-spot Catfish
- **Habitat:** West and Central African rivers
- **Length:** 200mm (8in)
- **Diet:** In common with most species of *Synodontis* that are not specialized feeders, this species will accept a wide variety of prepared and frozen foods.
- **Sex differences:** Not known
- **Aquarium compatibility:** An excellent community aquarium catfish well suited to small to medium-sized systems
- **Aquarium breeding:** Not known

Synodontis ocellifer is found in several colour forms. Some have large body spots and distinct pigment in the finnage; other populations are almost devoid of

Below: **Synodontis omias**
Although not well established in the fishkeeping hobby, this catfish is quite plentiful in the River Niger.

Above: **Synodontis petricolor**
An excellent dwarf catfish to include as part of a Rift Valley Lake cichlid community. Universally acclaimed for its handsome coloration.

body pigment but still possess the characteristic high, long-based adipose fin.

This catfish is sometimes available among West African shipments, although the large-spot form is quite rarely encountered by fishkeepers.

Synodontis omias
Brown Catfish
- **Habitat:** Niger River system
- **Length:** 430mm (17in)
- **Diet:** An omnivorous feeder, taking any type of aquatic insect and plant debris. All prepared and frozen foods are accepted
- **Sex differences:** Males possess a more slender body and less deep adipose fin in comparison with females
- **Aquarium compatibility:** Suitable for large-fish communities
- **Aquarium breeding:** Not known

During research into this species, the author discovered a close connection between the Brown Catfish and *Synodontis budgetti*, which may suggest that these fishes represent the male and female of one species of *Synodontis*.

Synodontis petricolor
Pygmy Catfish
- **Habitat:** Shoreline of Lake Tanganyika
- **Length:** 100mm (4in)
- **Diet:** Crustaceans
- **Sex differences:** Adult males are probably smaller (75mm/3in) than females
- **Aquarium compatibility:** Ideal for the miniature to large Rift Valley Lake cichlid community
- **Aquarium breeding:** Not known

Synodontis petricolor is perhaps one of the most beautiful species in this large genus. Its colour pattern is confusingly similar to the equally attractive Many-spotted Catfish, *Synodontis multipunctatus*, although the white borders to the fins are absent in the latter species.

The Pygmy Catfish is the smallest of the Rift Lake species and as such is perfect for most systems, although, sadly, it is very rarely available to fishkeepers.

Above: **Synodontis pleurops**
This young specimen displays all the features that make it such a popular catfish among aquarists. The large eye and long tail fin are familiar characteristics of the species. A very peaceful fish.

Synodontis pleurops
Big-eyed Catfish
- **Habitat:** Zaire
- **Length:** 300mm (12in)
- **Diet:** Insect larvae and algae
- **Sex differences:** Adult females are larger than males, and are usually drab in colour pattern
- **Aquarium compatibility:** Even large specimens are peaceful; an ideal catfish to keep among robust fishes
- **Aquarium breeding:** Not known

The Big-eyed Catfish has an ornate body pattern, which fades once it passes the half-grown stage. Adult specimens are somewhat drab in appearance, as the colour pattern darkens to a slate grey.

Even specimens 300mm (12in) long are compatible with small fishes, although by size alone they are bound to be disruptive in the majority of aquarium systems.

Synodontis robbianus
Brown-spotted Catfish
- **Habitat:** Niger River
- **Length:** 100mm (4in)
- **Diet:** Perhaps this species is a

semi-surface feeder in its natural habitat, as it is quick to take floating bloodworm and mosquito larvae when kept in the aquarium. A blend of dried flake and freeze-dried foods, together with frozen shrimp and insect larvae, will ensure this species thrives in captivity
- **Sex differences:** Females are deeper bodied than males
- **Aquarium compatibility:** Good community species, ideal for medium-sized aquariums
- **Aquarium breeding:** Not known

This small *Synodontis* could easily be confused with the more readily

Above: **Synodontis robbianus**
The leaf-brown body sets this fish apart from the grey of Synodontis nigrita; *both share a spotted skin.*

available *Synodontis nigrita*. It is much smaller in adult size, however, and has a longer adipose fin and a brown rather than grey body.

Synodontis robertsi
Tyson Robert's Catfish
● **Habitat:** Zaire River
● **Length:** 100-125mm (4-5in)
● **Diet:** In its native habitat, this species feeds on insect larvae and general organic debris. In the aquarium, it adapts to flake food, frozen bloodworm and shrimp
● **Sex differences:** Not known
● **Aquarium compatibility:** Excellent for small communities
● **Aquarium breeding:** Not known

The Robert's *Synodontis* was virtually unknown to enthusiasts until recently, when other species – notably *Synodontis caudalis* – had been confused with it. It is very similar to *S. alberti*, but has much more distinctive body blotches and is a smaller species.

Below: **Synodontis robertsi**
A half-grown specimen of one of the rarer Synodontis *species available.*

Above: **Synodontis schall**
Imported with Synodontis nigrita, *the white maxillary barbels and greyer body of this distinguish the two.*

Synodontis schall
Grey Catfish
- **Habitat:** West, Central and East Africa, in rivers and lakes
- **Length:** 430mm (17in)
- **Diet:** Insect larvae, insects, humus and algae
- **Sex differences:** Females are more robust and generally larger than males
- **Aquarium compatibility:** An aggressive species capable of stripping other fishes of their fins. Territorial among its own kind and towards other *Synodontis* species
- **Aquarium breeding:** Not known

Synodontis schall is the best-studied species within the genus, yet is probably one of the least suitable as an aquarium fish. In communities containing aggressive fishes, *Synodontis schall* can hold its own and will survive a very broad range of water conditions.

River Nile populations grow larger than Lake forms; a five-year-old fish from Lake Kainji in Nigeria measured 180mm (7in), whereas a fish of similar age from the River Nile in Sudan measured 390-400mm (15.4-16in). Almost 30 percent of the stomach contents in examined species consist of insect larvae, evidence of the dominant food source for *Synodontis* species.

Synodontis velifer
Velifer Catfish
- **Habitat:** West African rivers
- **Length:** 200mm (8in)
- **Diet:** Insect larvae, shrimp and prepared foods
- **Sex differences:** Not known
- **Aquarium compatibility:** A peaceful species suitable for most community systems
- **Aquarium breeding:** Not known

Synodontis velifer appears to be a relative newcomer to fishkeepers with a specialized interest in this genus. It is not clear in which area of Africa the few specimens available have originated, although the

Above: **Synodontis velifer**
The high dorsal fin is one of the most attractive features of this species.

original ones first encountered by scientists were collected in Ghana, from an Ashanti forest.

Wallago attu

Helicopter Catfish
- **Habitat:** Widely distributed in southern and Southeast Asia. Freshwater, but also found in tidal rivers in India, Pakistan, Burma, Thailand and Indochina
- **Length:** Up to 1.8m (6ft)
- **Diet:** Fish, crustaceans
- **Sex differences:** Not known
- **Aquarium compatibility:** Predatory towards small fishes, suitable for solitary isolation or among large robust fish
- **Aquarium breeding:** Not known

The Helicopter Catfish is imported among other Malayan catfishes and is usually purchased by an unsuspecting enthusiast. A night prowler, even small specimens can consume a great many fishes. Therefore, it should be kept only with fishes much larger than itself.

Below: **Wallago attu**
With the wide gape of a predator, this species will take small fishes.

Index to catfishes

Page numbers in **bold** indicate major references, including accompanying photographs. Page numbers in *italics* indicate other illustrations. Less important text entries are shown in normal type.

A

African Glass Catfish **46**
African Suckermouth Catfish **43,** 45
Albert's Catfish **57**
Angler Catfish **42**
Asian Glass Catfish *12*
Asian Red-tailed Catfish **53**
Asian Shark Catfish **54-5**
Auchenoglanis sp. 17, 24, 28
    occidentalis **40**

B

Bagridae 10, 36
Bagrids 17, 36
Bagarius 16, 24, 28, 40
    bagarius 29, **40**
Bagrus 28
Banded Catfish 58
Big-eyed Catfish **72**
Brachysynodontis batensoda
    Endpapers, **40-1**
Brichard's Catfish **58**
Brown Catfish **71**
Brown-spotted Catfish **73**
Bumblebee Catfish **48-9**

C

Chaca 24, 28
    bankanensis 42
    chaca 29, **42**
Chiloglanis 16, 22, 28, 45
    cameronensis 10, 29, **43**
Chrysichthys sp. 17, 28
    ornatus 29, **43**
Clarias 22, 23, 24, 28, 36
    batrachus 18, 29, **44**
Clarotes sp. 17, 28, **43**
    laticeps 29, **44-5**
Clown Catfish **61**
Crystal-eyed Catfish **54**

D

Dark-spotted Catfish **67-8**
Dark Synodontis **58**
Dwarf Giraffe Catfish **55**

E

Electric Catfish **51**
Euchilichthys 16
    guentheri 29, **45**
Eutropiellus debauwi 46
    vanderweyeri 15, 29, **46**

F

False Bumblebee Catfish **49**
False Chiloglanis **45**
False Chrysichthys **44-5**
False Nigriventris **58**
False Spotted Catfish **62-3**

False Suckermouth **45**
False Upside-down Catfish **67-8**
Feather Fin Catfish **63**
Filament Catfish **64**
Fischer's Catfish **56**
Frogmouth **42**
Fossil Catfish 47

G

Giant Flatmouth Catfish **40**
Giant Upside-down Catfish **40-1**
Giraffe-nosed Catfish **40**
Giraffe Synodontis **58-9**
Glass Catfish **48**
Glyptothorax 16, 22, 40
Greshoff's Catfish **65**
Grey Catfish **74**

H

Helicopter Catfish **75**
Hemisynodontis 41
    membranaceus 29, **46**
Heteropneustes fossilis **46-7**

K

Ko River Catfish **66**
Kryptopterus 24, 28
    bicirrhis 10, *12, 14,* 29, **48**

L

Large-spot Catfish **70-1**
Leiocassis sp. 13, 24, 28
    siamensis 14, 29, **48-9**
    stenomus 10, 29, **49**
Leopard Catfish **63**
Liver Catfish **46-7**
Lophiobagrus cyclurus 36, **50**

M

Malapterurus electricus 29, **51**
Malawi Catfish **69**
Many-spotted Catfish **66**
Mochokiella 28
    paynei 10, 29, *32,* **51**
Moustache Catfish **46**
Mystus sp. 13, 17, 24, 28, 29, 36
    armatus 37, **52**
    micracanthus 10, *14,* **52-3**
    nemurus **53**
    vittatus 37, **54**
    wykii **54**

O

One-spot Catfish **52, 69**
Ornate Catfish **43**

P

Pangasius 28
    sutchi 29, **54-5**
Parauchenoglanis macrostoma **55**
Payne's Catfish **51**
Pearl Catfish **52**
Phractocephalus 53
Polka-dot Catfish **57**
Pygmy Catfish **71**
Pygmy Leopard Catfish **63**

Pyjama Catfish **54**
Pyjamas Catfish **65**

R
Red-tailed Synodontis **60**
Robert's Synodontis **72**

S
Sisoridae Family 16
South American Red-tailed Catfish 53
Stinging Catfish **46-7**
Synodontis 10, 17, 24, *25*, 28, 29, 30, *33*,
  36, 37, 51, 57, 58, 59, 60, 62, 64, 65,
  69, 74
  afrofischeri 15, **56**
  alberti 15, **57**, 59, 72
  angelicus 57
  angelicus zonatus 57
  aterrimus 10, *15*, **58**
  brichardi 33, **58**
  budgetti 71
  camelopardalis **58-9**, 60
  caudalis 59, **60**, 72
  clarias 60
  decorus 58, **61**
  dhonti 30, **62-3**, 66
  eupterus 63
  eurystomus 10, 30, **63**, 66
  filamentosus **64**
  flavitaeniatus **65**
  greshoffi **65**
  koensis 66
  multipunctatus 15, 24, 30, 36, 37, *62*,
    63, **66-7**, 69, 71
  nigrita 63, **67-8**, *73*, 73, *74*
  nigriventris 10, 36, 58, **68**
  njassae 30, **69**
  notatus 69
  ocellifer Credits page, **70-1**
  omias 71
  petricolor 10, 30, 63, 66, **71**
  pleurops 72
  polli 63
  robbianus **72-3**
  robertsi 10, **60**, **73**
  schall 36, **74**
  tourei 66
  velifer **74-5**

T
Tanganyikan Dwarf Bagrid **50**
Two-spot Catfish **52-3**
Tyson Robert's Catfish **72**

U
Upside-down Catfish 58, 67, **68**

V
Velifer Catfish **74-5**

W
Walking Catfish **44**
Wallago 28
  attu 29, **75**
Whiptail Catfish **60**
Whiptail Synodontis **60**

Picture Credits

Artists
Copyright of the artwork illustrations on the pages following the artists' names is the
property of Salamander Books Ltd.
Clifford and Wendy Meadway: 11, 18, 19, 20(T), 24-5, 25, 26-7, 37

Colin Newman (Linden Artists): 16, 20(B)

Photographs
The publishers wish to thank the following photographers who have supplied
photographs for this book. The photographs have been credited by page number and
position on the page: (B) Bottom, (T) Top, (C) Centre, (BL) Bottom left, etc.
David Allison: 51(T), 55(T), 73(T)

Eric Crichton © Salamander Books Ltd: 21, 31

Lee Finley: 62(T)

Jan-Eric Larsson: 18, 42-3(T), 44, 48(T)

Arend van den Nieuwenhuizen: Title page, 46, 53(T), 68(T)

Bernard Pye: 16-7

Mike Sandford: 32, 67(T), 72(T)

David Sands: Endpapers, Credits page, 8-9, 14-5, 23, 33, 38-9, 40, 41, 42(B), 43, 45,
47, 48-9(C), 49(B), 50, 50-1(B), 52, 53(B), 54, 55(B), 56(T), 57, 58, 59, 60(B), 60-1(T),
61(B), 62(B), 63, 64, 65, 66, 67(B), 68(B), 69, 70, 71, 72-3(B), 74, 75

Jorg Vierke: 12

Keith Waller Associates © Salamander Books Ltd: 31

Rudolf Zukal: 56(B)

Acknowledgements
The publishers wish to thank Mr Peter Cottle for his help in preparing this book.

Brachysynodontis batensoda